WORKER PARTICIPATION: INDIVIDUAL CONTROL AND PERFORMANCE

WORKER PARTICIPATION: INDIVIDUAL CONTROL AND PERFORMANCE

DAVID GUEST AND DEREK FATCHETT

INSTITUTE OF PERSONNEL MANAGEMENT

Institute of Personnel Management
5 Winsley Street, Oxford Circus, London W1N 7AQ
First published 1974
© 1974 D E Guest and D J Fatchett

ISBN 0 85292 097 0

The case study on pp 156–7 is based on:

PAUL W J, ROBERTSON K B and HERZBERG F, Job Enrichment Pays Off, *Harvard Business Review*, March/April 1969

PAUL W J and ROBERTSON K B, *Learning from Job Enrichment*, Imperial Chemical Industries, 1969

PAUL W J and ROBERTSON K B, *Job Enrichment and Employee Motivation*, Gower Press, 1970

Made and printed in Great Britain by
The Garden City Press Limited
Letchworth, Hertfordshire
SG6 1JS

CONTENTS

CHAPTER ONE

INTRODUCTION: AN ANALYSIS OF PARTICIPATION

Society today reflects a number of pressures and conflicts. In particular, it reflects increasingly the conflict between the needs of the individual and the needs of a competitive and developing technology. There is a growing recognition that the individual has taken second place to the demands of technology. Many would argue that this has removed from the individual control over those factors that affect his life: the government of his country; his education; his leisure; his social relations; and his work.

A loss of control is reflected in a feeling of powerlessness which can be expressed in various ways – through withdrawal into apathy and inactivity; through a fixation on security and stability; through hitting out, often aimlessly, at anything that represents the 'system'; or through attempts to overthrow the 'system'. Among those who seek to adapt the present system, a major demand is for more opportunity for involvement and participation. By implication each of these becomes both a means and an end. Unfortunately, the loose way in which these concepts have been used has often rendered them virtually meaningless: nevertheless they are generally held to express something desirable. Asked whether they wanted to participate, most people will give a positive response.

Due largely to an increasing awareness of the need to make people feel a part of their social environment, participation has been a widely debated topic for a number of years. At the governmental level, the United Kingdom has seen pressures for greater local autonomy, particularly in Scotland and Wales. In the field of education, university students have won certain concessions over their right to have some say in important areas of decision-making. It is probably in the industrial context that the subject has been most widely examined in recent times. Europe as a whole has been rather more ready than the United Kingdom to innovate in this respect, with the systems of participation in West Germany and Yugoslavia being perhaps the most widely known. In contrast, the United Kingdom has seen certain informal attempts by groups of workers to exert control, the work-in at the Upper Clyde Shipbuilders providing probably the best known example. This has meant that the emphasis has been placed upon action rather than on the formal development of ideas.

In the industrial context, it would be incorrect to regard participation as a novel concept. The industrial history of the nineteenth century contains a series of ideas aimed at extending the participative functions of the workers. At one extreme, there were certain ideologies which called for a fundamental restructuring of the bases of society whilst, at the other, there were those which were satisfied with measures designed to ameliorate the conditions of the worker. Although producer-cooperatives, guild socialism, syndicalism and self-governing workshops never attracted more than minority support,[1] such ideas were powerful enough to form the basis of a near-continuous debate on the management of industrial organizations during the second half of the nineteenth century and the early years of this century.

More recently, interest in participation has been stimulated by the application to industry of psychological knowledge about the needs and motives of individuals, by a desire to discover new means of increasing productivity and by awareness of a possible Common Market directive on the subject. However, summarizing its attitude, the Royal Commission on Trades Unions and Employers Associations was not wholly enthusiastic: "the importance of the question of workers' participation in management for industrial relations is acknowledged, though any changes to encourage such participation should be subsidiary to reforms in collective bargaining" (1968, para 1105).* This would seem to reflect accurately the priorities of most trade unionists and employers, although it is quite legitimate to see collective bargaining as one form of participation. The Commission specifically did not recommend the appointment of worker directors; nevertheless, the Labour Government of the time permitted the newly formed British Steel Corporation to experiment with their use. The Government also initiated a major investigation into attitudes towards participation in another nationalized industry, British Rail.

Most of those who have been involved in participative programmes in industry and many of those who have written about them are understandably partisan in their views. Equally, others reject participation out of hand on purely ideological grounds. A debate involving the ideological and social issues of whether participation is a 'good thing' has sometimes clouded the issue of whether it is effective and what the criteria of effectiveness should be. By tradition and partly of necessity, most attempts at participation have been indirect, in that an individual participates through a representative. The alternative, which is often rejected as impracticable, but which might have far more potential where it can exist, is direct participation by each individual. Before examining these prospects any further, it is necessary to examine what is meant by participation.

PARTICIPATION – ITS MEANING

"Workers' participation in management is an old, persistent idea with many meanings." In these words, Walker and de Bellecombe (1967) summed up the problems surrounding an adequate definition of participation, although they did acknowledge that "the basic idea is obviously that the people who are managed should have some say about the decisions that affect them". The wide range of alternatives available makes the definition of participation in any study a

* All references are given in full at the end of the book.

matter of some considerable importance, since it is likely to determine the frame of reference for that particular study. In some cases, the term 'industrial democracy' has been used in preference to 'participation'; this probably reflects the orientation of the writers, but it need not necessarily have any significant impact on the analysis (see Emery and Thorsrud, 1969, Flanders, Pomeranz and Woodward, 1968).[2] Concentrating for the present on definitions of participation, one is struck by the frequent references to lower members of an organizational hierarchy having some 'say' or 'influence' over decision-making. French, Israel and Ås (1965), for instance, have described participation as "a process in which two or more parties influence each other in making certain plans, policies and decisions. It is restricted to decisions that have further effects on those making the decisions and on those represented by them".

Apart from the 'say' and 'influence', the other terms which are frequently mentioned are 'decision-making' and 'control' – Blumberg (1968, p 71), for example, writes "what I am primarily concerned with is decision-making by the workers. . . . I should like to include the entire spectrum of workers' power, from its most rudimentary form (receiving information from management) down to its opposite, complete worker determination."

Tannenbaum (1966) adopts a more specific definition of participation, referring to it as formal involvement of members in the exercise of control, usually through decision making in group meetings (p 85). Although this definition raises a number of questions, it does use control as its basis, with control being defined as "any process through which a person or a group of persons determines (ie intentionally effects) what another person or group of persons will do" (p 84).

To be of most value, any analysis must use a definition of participation which is measureable. 'Say' and 'influence' lack precision and would prove extremely difficult to quantify. The same can be said of 'sharing' unless the apportionments can be precisely specified. The spread of control in such a context can only be determined under conditions of opposition or conflict. If workers oppose something that management hopes to do and by so opposing cause the plans to be altered or abandoned, they would clearly be participating in the final decision. But this participation can only be shown to exist when a worker or group of workers attempts to exert control; that is, when they use their power.[3] In this context it is hard to see how certain forms of consultation or access to information constitute participation. The participation occurs when the workforce react in some way to the information, not when they are provided with information. The situation in which there is said to be a sharing of decision-making may be no more than a means whereby management controls the situation. The workforce are allowed a say as long as what they say has the agreement of management; when they disagree with management, then the say is taken away. Although it becomes a somewhat fine semantic point, 'control' is more precise and meaningful than a word like 'say' and has broader implications than 'decision-making'.

For these reasons, we would argue that a definition of participation which emphasizes control is most useful in any attempt to study participation objectively. Therefore, the potential for worker participation in management exists when the worker can exert his control. He may not in fact choose to exert his control but, unless that opportunity exists, only a form of pseudo-participation obtains whereby the worker is told that he may participate in management as long as his decisions are the same as those reached by the management. The definition of control suggested by Tannenbaum must be adapted slightly; he refers to determining the behaviour of other people: in the field of worker participation in management this must be extended to include decisions which determine the behaviour of oneself.

Using the concept of control as the key element in our definition of worker participation, in any analysis or evaluation of the subject it would seem to be necessary to examine those matters over which the worker attempts to seek control or accept control, his reasons for doing so and the results of his control. This has the advantage of being primarily based upon observable behaviour; furthermore, by posing the question 'why seek control?', it encourages an analysis of behaviour in terms of needs and motivation. Logically, this means that a phenomenon such as restriction of output, which is often seen as deviant by management, must be included as a form of participation.

An analysis in terms of control facilitates a discussion of the key issues related to participation. For example, participation is often seen as a threat to the authority of the manager. Within this framework, it is possible to examine the nature and extent of the control exerted by the various parties upon the decision-making process under different forms of participation. It also allows discussion of the argument that an increase in subordinate control necessarily leads to a lessening of superordinate control and hinders the achievement of managerial goals. Participation, then, will constitute the main theme of the book, and will be used to refer to those processes whereby subordinates are able to display an upward exertion of control. By subordinate, we mean those who do not have recognized authority in any particular relationship. This enables the foreman to be seen as a potential participant in his relationship with management, but as an authority figure in relation to those working under him. It is the nature of the relationship, rather than the level in the organizational hierarchy, that determines the potential participant.

THE ANALYSIS OF PARTICIPATION

Having defined participation in terms of control, it becomes apparent that the methods of control vary in form, level and purpose; it is therefore necessary to analyse these three key variables.

Forms of control

Collective bargaining, joint consultation, job enrichment and group decision-making are all potential forms of control over decision-making, yet there can be no doubt that there are fundamental differences between them. Discussing this problem, Lammers (1967) has suggested a useful distinction, and one that we shall follow, between 'direct' and 'indirect' forms of participation. "Indirect participation usually implies that the subordinate participants speak for their constituents with top managers about the general policy of the organization, procedures are formalized, and outside agencies often do influence to some extent what goes on. Direct participation, on the other hand, customarily entails that the subordinate participants speak for themselves about work or matters related to work; in general, aims, rules and means are not codified and external influences are normally absent."[4] This definition of direct participation, with individuals speaking for themselves, could be seen as emphasizing bargaining aspects. It therefore does not go far enough since direct participation also includes the possibility of the subordinate acting and taking decisions which influence his work, and which might normally be considered the prerogative of his superior. By implication, genuine forms of participation, both direct and indirect, must allow the individuals involved to take a decision in opposition to management; for example, the decision not to accept a change.

In the following chapters, we shall be concentrating almost exclusively upon direct forms of participation, although chapter 2 will look at the impact of indirect participation upon decision-making.

Level of participation

In any organization, and particularly a modern complex organization, a variety of decisions must be taken. These decisions can be conceived of as taking place at a variety of levels, mainly in terms of their impact on the organization. In this context, Walker (1970) has distinguished between four aspects of control:

(i) Ownership
(ii) Government of the enterprise

(iii) The process of management

(iv) Terms of employment.

Ownership and terms of employment are unambiguous categories. The other two categories described by Walker relate to a distinction which is often made in the analysis of management decision-making and in the role of organized labour in challenging such decisions. This is the distinction between legislative and executive decision-making. Whilst a hard and fast distinction cannot be maintained in a dynamic situation, it is desirable to recognize a degree of differentiation between decisions which are essentially concerned with how the enterprise shall pursue its objectives,[5] and those which are concerned with day to day situations and have to be resolved within the established administrative framework. The executive level of decision-making will include decisions relating to the performance of tasks, and the degree of control that the individual is able to exert. It might also logically include decisions concerned with terms of employment which Walker sees as a separate category.

Within these broad levels, there exist several types of participation designed to control and influence the output of the decision-making process (see Table 1). Normally, the direct forms of participation will fall into the category of executive decisions directly related to task performance.

Table 1

Level of decision making

Level	Forms of participation
Legislative	Worker directors
Executive—not directly related to task performance	Collective bargaining Joint consultation
Executive—directly related to task performance	Job enrichment Restriction of output

Orientations to participation

The third important variable we have suggested as necessary for the analysis of a participative situation relates to the definitions of participation held by the actors within a particular context; that is to say, the purpose they attach to participation. To facilitate an understanding of such definitions, we intend to hypothesize two basic orientations, which can be seen as representing the extremes of a continuum of attitudes towards participation. Some of the attitudes touched upon here will be extended in chapter 4, when four distinct managerial ideologies and their importance to participation will be discussed. For the present we will draw a broad distinction between what can be called the distributive and integrative orientations.

The major characteristics of the distributive orientation can be summarized in the following way:

1 It is argued that the workers and their representatives have insufficient power and are manipulated by managers and owners alike to achieve goals over which they have little or no control. This feeling of powerlessness has been reinforced in recent years by the increasing pace of technological and social changes and has sometimes resulted in redundancies and the abolition of traditional working practices. To counter this trend, a broader distribution of control within organizations is called for. For example, the Labour Party document, *Industrial Democracy* (1967) stressed the need for increased workers' control over financial, commercial and manpower matters.

2 Within capitalist societies, conflict, latent or manifest, is considered an inevitable characteristic of any business organization, since the members of that organization have potentially differing goals and aspirations. Therefore the favoured forms of participation will be conflict-based, with the objective of thereby extending the frontiers of control.

3 Forms of participation that are not directly aimed at

increasing the amount of workers' control will generally be rejected. This is well illustrated by the following quotation from a symposium of papers on workers' control: "Participation is the catchword of the Right. This phrase covers a multitude of proposals and suggestions aimed at diverting the worker's struggle to extend his rights into safe channels. Basically, it aims to create a façade to give the impression that worker's representatives at a number of levels have been party to decision-making. The objective is clear. It is to commit the workers to policies decided by management and thus, if not to eliminate, at least to reduce and mute the struggle against them" (Ramelson, 1970).

In contrast, the integrative orientation has the following characteristics:

1 Participation is seen as a method of increasing organizational efficiency. It is hoped that by ceding a degree of control to the workers, decisions will become effectuated. In particular, by involving the worker in decisions about task performance, it is expected that he will be more highly motivated to accept organizational goals. This suggested relationship between motivation and increased organizational efficiency has been depicted by Lammers (1967, p 210) in the following rather simplistic way:

Figure 1

'Power Raise' for Lower Ranks
↓
Increase in Employee Motivation   Upward Communication of Relevant Information
↓
Increase in Total Amount of Power[6]   ↑

2 Conflict is regarded as either irrelevant or of minimal importance to the effective functioning of a participative system. The organization is seen as having rationally defined objectives, and the aim is to stimulate a consen-

sual acceptance of objectives; consequently, any form of conflict is seen as being largely irrational. To use Fox's (1970) terminology, the organization is perceived in unitary terms with only one source of authority and loyalty.

3 The favoured forms of participation are direct and task-related. The job content is seen as capable of stimulating satisfaction and motivation: this constitutes the beginning of the motivational chain and it is hoped it will lead to increased organizational efficiency.

The need to differentiate between the purposes attached to participation has been noted by a number of writers. For instance, Child (1969) has seen those who support forms of participation which embrace both the determination of business goals and the means of achieving them, a representing a left-wing, non-managerial viewpoint. On the other hand, those who restrict the content of participation to the determination of means tend to have another and distinctly managerial perspective. These differences are illustrated by Child (1969, p 89) in the following form, although we have added the examples:

Table 2

Scope of decision-making

		Goals + Means *(Democratic)*	Means only
Focal level	Whole organization	*Type A* (Yugoslav experiment in workers' council)	*Type B* (Joint consultation)
	Small group or individual[8]	*Type D* (Self-governing workgroup)[7]	*Type C* (Job enrichment)

Walker (1970) in a more detailed analysis of the role of participation has isolated nine perspectives or attitudes towards participation, not all of which are in favour of it. Attitudes are inevitably linked with the perceived purpose and this in turn is linked to the type of participation. The attitudes held by managers and workers are analysed separately in later sections; at this stage, it is possible to isolate four major objectives which are likely to be linked to direct forms of participation.

1 Increased productivity or efficiency. This is primarily a managerial objective and exists on the assumption that the full potential contribution of the workforce has not been tapped in the past and will be utilized to a greater extent through participation.

2 Increased worker satisfaction. Although this rather begs the question of what constitutes worker satisfaction, the assumption is that either the process of participation or the rewards of the participative effort will result in greater satisfaction. This is an end in itself for the work force whilst management will undoubtedly look for additional spin-offs.

3 Reduced industrial conflict. Industrial conflict is, in itself, a direct form of participation. However, management will be looking for a reduction in conflict, in association with an increase in job satisfaction.

4 Increased industrial democracy. A number of people, including some who are not directly involved in industry, see this as an end in itself. Discussion of this aspect of participation is highly value laden and we do not intend to discuss it in full. Two lines of reasoning emerge: one stresses the need to maintain some sort of equilibrium in which the interests of all 'stake-holders' (Rhenman, 1969) are represented and protected. The other suggests that this type of democracy reduces alienation and brings about a feeling of involvement.

In the subsequent chapters, the impact of the various forms

of participation will be evaluated in the context of these main purposes or objectives. It will become clear that, in general, objective evidence has only been collected in relation to productivity and job satisfaction, and therefore the emphasis will be placed on these.

THE FOCUS ON DIRECT PARTICIPATION

As we have already said, this book is primarily concerned with the direct forms of participation and constitutes an attempt both to analyse and evaluate them. We have chosen to concentrate on the direct rather than the indirect forms of participation for a number of reasons. It is clear that the major debates on worker participation have been and will probably continue to be concerned with the indirect forms. For its part, management in the United Kingdom has been showing increasing signs of dissatisfaction with the indirect forms of participation and particularly with the fragmentation of collective bargaining. One result was the pressure which led to the Industrial Relations Act of 1971. Another has been the search for alternative means of managing the workforce which both avoid the expense of conflict and provide an outlet for the needs of the workers without increasing labour costs. For a while, management turned to productivity bargaining as a palliative. By highlighting the scope for improvement it led some to question the competence of managers who had continued to tolerate inefficiencies for so long. It also extended the frontiers of control for a number of workers. Another alternative was to turn more consciously towards certain of the direct forms of participation, particularly those advocated by a number of organizational psychologists. Since productivity bargaining has tended to fall out of favour, there is every reason to believe that, under normal economic conditions, management interest in the direct forms of participation will continue to increase. There is therefore a need to understand the thinking of the advocates of these strategies, a need to examine how they operate in practice and a need to evaluate their effectiveness in the light of a number of possible objectives. For management, the central concern must be the impact on organizational effectiveness that results from giving some control to the worker.

Another reason for this particular focus is that certain forms of direct participation are considered by some to provide the best means of countering the trends in technology which are said to be 'unhealthy' for both the individual and society. It is important to present these viewpoints, avoiding the emotion which they often arouse, and to ask whether or not they are realistic. Again, much of the relevant literature has been value-laden because it has sought to present a particular point of view. Still more has been written with a primary objective of impressing industrialists in an area which can provide lucrative consultancy work. Therefore considerable care must be taken to evaluate correctly the true worth of evidence presented in this context.

The effects of technology on the workplace are widely considered to be alienating. It is argued that workers perceive or are aware of this and many writers on direct participation assume this to be so. Others have argued against this assumption and made it clear that it is necessary to find out whether the workers really do feel alienated and whether they want to participate. (See, for example C Wright Mills, 1957; Goldthorpe *et al*, 1968). Some attention will be given, therefore, to the attitudes of the workers towards participative concepts.

An important though often neglected constraint on any analysis of the implications for the United Kingdom is that much of the better known work in this area has been carried out in America and to a lesser extent in Europe. Yet cultural and environmental differences can have a major influence on the impact of this type of approach. Therefore, although this work will be included, greater emphasis will be given to work conducted in the United Kingdom; and without necessarily always diminishing their relevance for Europe and America, the implications arising out of experience of direct participation are considered with the United Kingdom in mind. For the same reason, the following chapter on indirect forms of participation focuses only upon those forms already operating in the United Kingdom.

Finally, a considerable amount of information relating to the direct forms of participation is available in the literature. However, little of it has been brought together in a coherent manner. The fields of industrial psychology, industrial sociology, management and industrial relations are too often kept distinct; also, a wide gap often exists between the researcher and the practitioner. (Williams and Guest, 1969). An attempt is made in this book to bring together, within a coherent framework, the relevant ideas and research evidence.

Summary

Interest in participation has been growing in recent years, partly because it is seen as a response, and sometimes a solution, to certain pressures within society. In the industrial context, despite its long history, it has often proved difficult to analyse satisfactorily, often as a result of the loose way in which it has been defined. In this chapter we have focused upon control and defined worker participation as a process whereby subordinates are able to display an upward exertion of control. The nature of this control will be determined by three key variables.

1 The form of participation. A distinction between direct and indirect forms of participation has been introduced. In direct participation, each worker can take decisions and exert control; with indirect participation, this is done on his behalf by a representative. This book is mainly concerned with direct participation.

2 The content of participation. Participation can be concerned with the ownership and government of an enterprise. It generally focuses upon either legislative decisions, such as those concerning the terms and conditions of employment, or upon executive decisions,

which relate to the day to day running of the enterprise. The emphasis throughout will be on executive decisions and particularly on those relating to task performance.

3 The purpose of participation. A basic distinction has been drawn between those who adopt a distributive and an integrative orientation. The distributive orientation views conflict as inevitable, and calls for a more even distribution of power between management and worker and rejects forms of participation which try to evade these issues. The integrative orientation minimizes the significance of conflict and views participation as a means of increasing job satisfaction and productivity. Direct forms of participation are more often associated with the integrative viewpoint and lead to four main objectives: increased job satisfaction, increased productivity, improved industrial relations and increased industrial democracy.

Recent dissatisfaction with indirect forms of participation is encouraging a number of managers to pay more attention to the direct forms. Assessments of their impact can sometimes prove difficult because much of the writing is value-laden or has appeared in a different context. For these and other reasons, this book will attempt to analyse and evaluate the direct forms of participation.

NOTES

1 See S and B Webb (1920, p 650), who claimed that in the evidence presented to the 1891–94 Royal Commission on Labour, there was "absolutely no claim, and no suggestion, that trade unions should participate in the direction of industry". Also, Coates and Topham (1968) and Clarke, Fatchett and Roberts, (1972).
2 Tabb and Goldfarb's (1970) approach depends upon the development of a framework for analysis rather than concentrating upon an objective definition of participation. (This can be used as a basis for comparison between different case studies of participation. It could also be used by researchers who want to adopt a social action perspective thereby constructing models of participation based upon the definitions held by the actors.)
3 Power can be defined as "the ability or capacity to exercise control". (Tannenbaum, 1966, p 84).
4 'General Policy' is used in the consultative sense, where policy issues are mainly discussed in a historical perspective.
5 For instance, decisions concerned with major investment programmes, rationalization and commercial policy.
6 Lammers argues that it is possible to increase the overall total of control within an organization. This means that the ceding of control to the subordinate does not involve a diminution of control by the superordinates. Tannenbaum (1966) has provided evidence which indicates that this holds true at the perceptual level.
7 See H A Clegg, *A New Approach to Industrial Democracy*, Blackwell, Oxford, 1960.
8 Individual has been added to the original diagram, since, for example, Herzberg (1959, 1966) stresses the limited relevance of groups in effectively motivating behaviour.

CHAPTER TWO

PARTICIPATION: THE INDIRECT FORMS OF CONTROL

Participation has been defined as the upward exertion of control by subordinates over various forms of organizational activity, with that control being exercised directly by the worker himself, or indirectly through some means of representation. It is the intention of this chapter to examine the indirect systems of control that have developed in the industrial context in the United Kingdom. Collective bargaining and joint consultation are now established as the dominant means of indirect participation within the enterprise. The other form of participation which is considered in this chapter and which for some time has been a focus of attention in certain Western European countries is the acceptance of a number of worker directors on the board of companies.[1] Building upon the framework of control already suggested, it becomes necessary to discuss:

1 the extent of control over managerial decisions resulting from worker directors, collective bargaining and joint consultations; and
2 (as we are dealing with indirect forms of participation) the extent of control achieved by the represented over his representative.

COLLECTIVE BARGAINING

According to the Ministry of Labour's Handbook (1961, p 8), "the term collective bargaining is applied to those arrangements, under which wages and conditions of employment are settled by a bargain in the form of an agreement between employers or associations of employers and workers' organizations". Our present concern is wider than the determination of wages and working conditions as we are interested in all those aspects of management over which the bargaining process exerts an influence. For purposes of analysis and description, a distinction will be made between those areas of bargaining that are accepted as legitimate by the actors and those where workers, to use Goodrich's (1920) concept, seek to establish new frontiers of control. These new frontiers of control will necessitate inroads into traditional managerial prerogatives.

Until the mid 1950s, the locus of power in relation to collective bargaining was rooted at the industry level, and opportunities for indirect participation by work-based union representatives in the determination of wages and conditions were limited, although they did exist. Groups of workers, or even individuals, were often able to bargain about overtime and prices under an incentive scheme. Also, it must be recognized that industry-wide agreements provided procedures for the processing of individual grievances, and group bargaining activities could be built around these arrangements.

From the mid 1950s onwards, there has been a marked shift in emphasis towards the acceptance of the plant or the company as the context in which industrial relations are more effectively conducted. Roberts and Gennard (1970), grouped the factors responsible for this growth under three main headings: (a) economic, (b) institutional and (c) role of the government. Of these, the establishment and continuation of near-full employment in the 1950s and 1960s, resulting in increased trade union power and the subsequent emphasis upon productivity, have generally been recognized as the most important. The growth in significance of intra-plant activities is indicated by the composition of earnings in many industries (Donovan Report, p 12), the extended use of procedure agreements (Marsh and McCarthy, 1968), and the centrality of the role of the shop steward. On this point, Marsh and Coker (1963, p 177) have estimated a 72 per cent increase in the number of recognized shop stewards in federated engineering establishments between May 1947 and December 1961. Equally, the Government Social Survey (1968, p 86) found that 70 per cent of the managers interviewed preferred to deal with shop stewards, rather than full-time trade union officials. This figure increased to 80 per cent for those in metal handling industries. This preference can be attributed to the more intimate knowledge of the steward, and the possibility that his continued involvement could lead to a speedier settlement of the problem.

Summarizing the present nature of plant bargaining, Goldthorpe *et al* (1968, p 170) have drawn attention to four characteristics:

(i) "that the number of shop stewards relative to union members is growing, and also the extent to which shop stewards are involved in bargaining procedures;
(ii) "that systems of workplace industrial relations are developing spontaneously on a wide scale, and are operating in a largely self-contained and self-regulating manner;
(iii) "that for a large majority of union members, the steward is the union; and
(iv) "that most members feel relatively satisfied with the way in which workshop unionism and bargaining actually function."

With the possible exception of productivity bargaining, the trend towards plant and company level bargaining has not radically altered the traditionally accepted scope of the processes. Wages and working conditions have provided and continue to provide the main area of control; 73 per cent of the shop stewards interviewed in the Government Social Survey sample discussed and settled items relating to working conditions as standard practice; 56 per cent were similarly involved with wages issues. In addition to these topics, it became clear that between one-third and one-half of the shop stewards were more or less regularly involved in determining hours of work, discipline and employment issues (defined to include taking on new labour, number of apprentices, acceptance of up-grading, short time and redundancy questions).

The picture of a narrow and specific context for collective bargaining was altered with the advent of productivity bargaining. Managements, it was argued, had lost control over wage payment systems and working methods on the shop floor and, in order to regain control, it was necessary to share a range of decisions with representatives of the workers. Reviewing the Fawley productivity agreements, Flanders (1964, p 234) was prepared to assert that "management was in no position to impose its will simply by claiming the right to manage". Alternatively, this did not mean that productivity bargaining meant an abdication of managerial responsibilities; on the contrary, the success of most productivity agreements depended upon managements being prepared to work out in detail all the implications of the envisaged changes and put forward practical proposals.

It is not the purpose of this particular study to argue the merits of this type of bargaining whose growth, to cover approximately six million or about 25 per cent of all employed workers by the end of June 1969 (National Board for Prices and Incomes [NBPI], 1969, p 3), was attributable largely to Government interest in incomes policy and a need to relate wage increases to productivity in a period of full employment. Its subsequent decline in popularity can be related to a sharp increase in unemployment, which has increased workers' needs for security, whilst at the same time extending managers' ability to take unilateral decisions. The importance of productivity bargaining in relation to participation was to be found in the potential provided for workers to exert greater control over decision-making. No longer was collective bargaining narrowly defined to include simply wages and working conditions, but it had been extended to cover a whole range of topics concerned with the planning and utilization of labour. This meant that working practices, rules and customs, levels of overtime, and the use of plant and machinery were accepted as areas for bargaining, in an attempt by managements to remove impediments to increased productivity. Nevertheless, a study by Clarke, Fatchett and Roberts (1972), which attempted to estimate workers' influence upon certain types of decision, would seem to suggest that joint regulation of decisions relating to the use of labour is extremely rare. Even more limited is the degree of influence over capital decisions such as investment and distribution of profits.

A fairly common feature of productivity bargaining was the establishment of joint committees to evaluate and monitor agreements, and to oversee the use of techniques involved in implementation. This resulted in an emphasis upon training shop stewards in managerial techniques such as job evaluation, work study and method study, as well as certain elements of accountancy. For instance, a productivity agreement concluded at the Steel Company of Wales plant at Port Talbot had provisions for formal joint committees to deal with job evaluation, training, the financing of the agreement, and disputes arising out of the interpretation of the agreement. (Owen-Smith, 1971).

With this often extensive involvement arising during the course of negotiating and implementing the agreement, a certain paradox became apparent. Workers' maintenance of impediments to optimum efficiency had created a bargaining position from which it was possible to exert a price for their potential relaxation. Yet one of the managerial aims in initiating productivity discussions had been to regain control over the production process and the payment system, thereby ostensibly eliminating the means by which workers had been able to influence managerial decisions. For instance, Flanders (1966, p 6) saw the plant productivity agreement as "a logical first step towards a modern viable system of managerial control over pay and effort."[2] It follows from this that, despite the seemingly participative nature of productivity bargaining, the implementation of such agreements might result in a decrease, rather than an increase, in future possibilities for participation, unless specific provision is made for the joint regulation of the agreement. Because of this, the Transport and General

Workers Union [TGWU] has argued that productivity agreements do not constitute a once-for-all bargain, but "a continuous process of bargaining in which the union keeps open all its options to deal with new circumstances and opportunities for gain for its members as and when they arise" (*Incomes Data*, 1970, p 23). The areas covered by productivity bargaining and more particularly the attempt to establish the principle of mutuality and joint regulation represent a challenge to existing frontiers of control.

"The productivity agreement has been and is often conceived as a wage–work bargain in which changes in methods of working are negotiated in conjunction with increases in remuneration. The immediate aim of the agreement is to restrain or reduce labour costs thereby increasing labour productivity immediately and in the longer term." (Daniel, 1970, p 24). In addition to this initial aim, Daniel lists possible indirect effects of productivity agreements: on the attitudes and expertise of managers, on the attitudes and job satisfaction of operators, on the roles of trade unions and their full-time and lay officers, and on the institutions and climate of industrial relations. Of particular relevance in the present context was the impact of productivity agreements on job satisfaction. Daniel examined productivity agreements in a petro-chemical plant and in a nylon spinning plant, and in both cases found an increase in job satisfaction.

In the petro-chemical plant, the most frequently mentioned source of satisfaction with the agreement was the way in which job changes had increased interest and satisfaction at work by providing workers with greater opportunity to use their abilities in learning and carrying out a wider range of jobs, both simple maintenance tasks and operating jobs covering a broader span of the process. Over two-thirds of the sample spontaneously mentioned this aspect of the change as a source of satisfaction with the agreement.

The management of the nylon spinning plant attempted to use the productivity bargain not only to achieve the conventional objectives but also to introduce job enrichment. Because of technological constraints, Daniel preferred to use the term job extension rather than job enrichment. Nevertheless, "62 per cent of the men said that their job had become more interesting as a result of changes that the agreement brought about. This majority is substantially smaller than the ones favouring changes in work group and supervisory relations and, moreover, the way they developed their reasons for saying this shows that what is meant was that the work was less boring rather than more interesting, less a source of deprivation rather than becoming a source of positive gratification. The work had become less boring, but it remained a fundamentally uninteresting set of tasks." (1970, p 76).

These two examples are not included to suggest that every productivity agreement led to an increase in worker job satisfaction, or that expectations in relation to sources of satisfaction and deprivation are determined wholly or mainly within the workplace. But they do serve to show that, when we are considering indirect forms of participation, we must be conscious of their potential impact on the worker's task environment.

Consistent with the TGWU demands for joint regulation of productivity agreements are the increasing pressures from shop stewards to widen the scope of topics deemed suitable for the bargaining process. In the Government Social Survey sample of shop stewards, 76 per cent thought there were issues which should be discussed jointly with management but which the latter generally considered as their own prerogative. Implicitly, the extension of bargaining questions involves a challenge to doctrines of managerial prerogatives and this becomes apparent when one examines the list of topics that stewards saw as suitable for joint regulation: 25 per cent mentioned financial policy of the company, 23 per cent rights of dismissal and discipline and 17 per cent production, new methods, machinery and efficiency (the demand for *status quo* clauses in procedure agreements would mean that all changes envisaged by managements would have to be jointly discussed). Similarly, a Labour Party (1967) document, *Industrial Democracy*, suggested that the frontiers of control be redefined to include redundancy, manpower planning, discipline, manning and labour utilization as areas of joint determination. "This widening of the subject matter has the important consequence that it calls not only for the periodic renegotiation or reshaping of agreements but also requires the development of more continuous systems of joint regulation or joint determination." (Labour Party, 1967, p 38).

The document argued that joint determination involved no encroachment upon trade union freedom and control over management, as long as the right of withdrawal from agreements was maintained. Nevertheless, the establishment of new areas of control, and the consequent involvement in decision making, are viewed both with concern and enthusiasm in trade union circles. On the one hand, there are those who argue that unionists should aim to participate in and control the management of enterprises in which they work, whilst others feel that collective bargaining freedom is of paramount importance and that participation necessarily imposes constraints upon freedom. The earlier-cited TGWU demand for joint determination falls into the first category, with the Electrical Trades Union's (1966) outright rejection of participative systems, other than wage bargaining providing an example of the second. Discussion around these two models of trade union functions has a sound historical basis amongst those influential in the labour movement, and represents an important divergence in ideology. Nevertheless, it is of some interest to note that until Goldthorpe *et al* (1968) asked questions related to this area, the ordinary members' perception of trade union functions had scarcely been elicited; 52 per cent of the 'affluent' workers in that study agreed with the view that "unions should first be concerned with getting higher pay and better conditions"; in contrast, 40 per cent felt that "unions should also try to get a say in management". Although those in favour of extended trade union functions were in a minority overall, they formed 61 per cent of the skilled workers. Summarizing their findings, the authors concluded that the workers favoured a 'limited-function' trade union – "the union, that is, which concentrates its activities almost exclusively on their economic protection and advancement". (1968, p 109).

In the early 1970s the strength of the demands to redefine the frontiers of control would appear to be both gaining ground and at the same time to be under attack. Behaviour within the industrial relations system increasingly reflects the perceived conflict between values of efficiency, and of what might be termed democracy in so far as they assert the workers' right to control decision-making. The need for predictability and efficiency in industrial relations was one of the factors leading to the Industrial Relations Act 1971. Whilst radically restructuring the voluntary system of industrial relations, it could at the same time push back the frontiers of control by making practices such as the closed shop and sympathy strikes illegal. On the other hand, workers have demanded the right to challenge and veto decisions relating to the utilization of both labour and capital. The use of the sit-in and work-in, particularly when closure is threatened, constitutes evidence of action to meet this demand. In a more specific way, access to information has been recognized by representatives of differing viewpoints as an essential prerequisite to participation. For instance, the Code of Practice (1971) recommended that "management should aim to meet all reasonable requests from trade unions for information which is relevant to the negotiations in hand" (para 97). A subsequent Commission on Industrial Relations [CIR] report (Report No 31, 1972) offered no explicit advice as to the type of information that should be given to workers' representatives: it would seem that the more detailed items in that report would not satisfy the desire for information that has arisen in situations of direct action. Our analysis points to an increasing conflict between these two sets of values. Recognition of this conflict is reflected in the debate within the Labour Party about

. .

the re-structuring of the ownership of key sections of industry.

JOINT CONSULTATION

Formal joint consultation, which can be seen as any method of establishing two-way communications between management and workers in addition to those provided by normal day to day contact, constitutes a second major form of indirect participation. The objectives of joint consultation have never been closely defined by its advocates; nevertheless, it is possible to discern three arguments that are generally mentioned:

1 that joint consultation would enhance the achievement of increased productivity by involving the workers, through their representatives, in the planning of the production process;

2 that joint consultation would provide a channel of communication, thereby lessening the mistrust and suspicion of the workers towards management's plans and objectives; and

3 that joint consultation would ensure for the workers a voice in the management of the enterprise. In this way, a moral right would be satisfied, and increased cooperation and efficiency would result.

These points highlight the close association of joint consultation with the integrative orientation outlines in chapter 1. Such an approach seemed particularly relevant in the immediate post-war conditions, and, at that time, consultation underwent a period of considerable popularity. In a study conducted in the late 1940s, the National Institute for Industrial Psychology [NIIP] (1951) found that 545 out of 751 firms replying to their questionnaire had some machinery for joint consultation. In contrast, Clarke, Fatchett and Roberts (1972) found that only 32 per cent of their respondents had a formally constituted body used solely for consultation. Nevertheless, that study did find that larger organizations exhibited a greater propensity to possess

33

consultative bodies. Only 17·6 per cent of the firms employing fewer than 500 had formalized committees, compared with 57·7 per cent of those organizations employing more than 1,000.

It is now firmly accepted that there has been a significant decline in interest in joint consultation. For instance, Clarke, Fatchett and Roberts found a higher degree of expressed dissatisfaction with consultative machinery than with negotiating bodies. (See also A I Marsh and E E Coker, 1973, who found a reduction of one-third in the number of joint production committees in federated engineering establishments between 1955 and 1961.) We consider that there are three principal reasons accounting for this relative lack of interest:

1 The type of topics discussed have been largely of an historical and non-contentious nature, and this has limited the possibilities of workers' representatives being involved in decisions of real concern to their members.
2 The growth of plant bargaining, including the variant of productivity bargaining, has provided a major outlet for joint decision-making on matters of significance to the workers.
3 Managements have continued to adopt the practice of communicating directly with the workers, rather than relying upon workers' representatives. The emphasis has been placed upon the management hierarchy, particularly the supervisor, as the means of communication. Anthony (1970) noted, in his study of the National Coal Board, a strong tendency on the part of management to by-pass the consultative machinery. Some recent industrial disputes have been notable for a tendency for management to communicate directly to their workers, rather than through recognized trade union officials.

Studies of consultation by the NIIP (1951), and Anthony (1970) support the viewpoint that the topics discussed are mainly historical and non-contentious. To a certain extent, this must necessarily be the case, as traditional areas of trade

34

union activity – wages and working conditions – are specifically excluded from discussion by the constitution of many joint consultative committees.

In his study of consultation at various levels in the National Coal Board, Anthony divided the topics discussed into ten main areas—seven of which he saw as matters of recorded performance, and the other three as matters concerning change and innovation.

Matters of recorded performance	*Matters concerning change and innovation*
1 Production performance	1 Production changes
2 Situation of the industry	2 Manpower changes
3 Manpower records	3 Training changes
4 Safety and health	
5 Training reports	
6 Joint consultation	
7 General	

Significantly, Anthony found that the most discussed topics – production performance, manpower records and safety and health – contained a heavy historical content and were generally non-contentious. The impression gained by the study was that management regarded consultative meetings as an opportunity to communicate and inform, and great care was taken to avoid topics that might generate conflict and challenge management's right to make decisions. The problems surrounding change, which might have proved to be more conflict prone, were generally left untouched.

In contrast to joint consultation with its rather limited opportunities for workers' representatives to be involved in matters of concern, plant bargaining ensured for the shop steward the role of joint decision-maker. We have traced already the importance of plant bargaining in changing the locus of power in the negotiating context; it had additional significance in establishing an effective challenge to joint consultation, both as a method of regulating industrial relations within the plant and as a device to attract workers' loyalty and interest. Although too great an emphasis is often placed on the cash nexus between the workers and the firm, it could be argued that joint consultation did not stress this element sufficiently to divert attention towards taking an overall interest in the prosperity of the firm. Yet productivity bargaining, which has covered certain traditional consultative topics, has succeeded in attracting greater worker interest, largely as a result of the generally associated cash incentive. According to one viewpoint (McCarthy, 1966) joint consultation in the strict sense cannot survive the development of effective shop floor organization.

The contrasting fortunes of joint consultation and collective bargaining in the past offer useful indicators to the possible success of these and other forms of participation in the future. For example, they suggest that participation must be concerned with matters of real interest to the worker. Naturally enough, wages and working conditions have always been such matters and, of necessity, have formed the basis of collective bargaining. A key issue, therefore, is whether the interests of workers are likely to extend to topics covered by forms of direct participation. There is evidence to suggest that managements need the cooperative involvement of the workers to achieve a whole range of organizational goals and that, at the same time, workers' representatives are pressing for more aspects of management to be jointly regulated through the bargaining process. A combination of these two forces could lead to the increasing dominance of collective bargaining and to a further extension of the topics covered by it.

WORKER REPRESENTATION IN GOVERN-MENTAL BODIES WITHIN THE ENTERPRISE

In this country, procedures to ensure worker participation on the boards of companies have existed in only a limited number of cases. (See examples listed in the *Observer*, 5.4.70). That is not to say that there has been a lack of interest in participation at this level. (See, for instance, Trades Union

Congress [TUC] 1966 evidence to Donovan Commission.) The composition of boards in nationalized concerns provided a potent source of controversy within the labour movement during the 1920s and 1930s, with the conflict being finally resolved by a joint decision of the Labour Party and the TUC in 1935. This decision guaranteed that a right of representation for workers' organizations on the governing bodies of any nationalized industry would be secured by statute. (Labour Party Annual Conference Report, 1935.) Neverthelesss, board members were to be appointed according to efficiency and competence criteria, although it was acknowledged that experience in labour organizations might constitute sufficient evidence of competence. This approach was adopted in the legislation which led to the nationalization of various industries in the post-1945 period. Full-time board members, appointed as a result of their trade union experience, were in a minority. Generally, they came from different industries, and were expected to give up trade union office. It is noticeable that the whole debate related to nationalized industries; there was no mention of private enterprise.

Against this background, the appointment in 1968 by the British Steel Corporation [BSC] of 12 employee directors to their board structure represented a significant innovation, as it marked a new conception of worker representation at the governmental level of the enterprise. Hitherto, worker representatives on the boards of nationalized industries had been required to possess special knowledge of the frame of reference and needs of the ordinary employee, without necessarily having to work in the industry. For the BSC experiment, employment within the Corporation was essential, thereby allowing the worker representatives to be drawn from a wide range of jobs as well as facilitating the maintenance of contact with fellow workers and attendance at trade union meetings. Although the experiment constituted an innovation in participation for a major organization in the United Kingdom, the BSC considered it to be no more than supplementary to the traditional process of bargaining and consultation.

At the time of writing, the BSC is organized into six product divisions, with each division having its own non-statutory board of directors. The employee directors sit on these divisional boards in an advisory capacity. As the divisional managing directors are solely responsible for decisions, the boards do not vote. Product divisions are not solely responsible for certain decisions, particularly those concerned with development and closure of plants, and this results in an additional limitation upon the extent of participation. These decisions must be referred to the national board of the Corporation, on which there are no employee directors.

The first evaluation (Brannen *et al*, 1972) of the experiment indicated trends that are not significantly different from overseas experience. For instance, those who have attempted evaluations of the German system of co-determination are fairly consistent in asserting that the scheme has made little difference, whether judged in terms of efficiency, industrial relations or job satisfaction. In his evidence to the Donovan Commission, Turner (1966), went as far as to say that co-determination had made no difference (p 12). Certainly it does not seem to have given the ordinary worker a sense of participating; studies reported by Für-stenberg (1969) found that, although about three-quarters of the workers knew that co-determination had been introduced into their enterprise, "only half of the inter-viewed workers had any concrete ideas about the actual meaning of co-determination" (p 130). A more extreme example is provided by Neuloh (1960), who found that in one big firm in the Ruhr only 14 of the 733 workers interviewed had any detailed knowledge of the working of co-determination.

Reviewing the Norwegian experience of employee directors in certain state-owned industries, Emery and Thorsrud (1969, p 83) drew the following conclusion about the employee directors' ability to further the interests of their fellow workers:

"When we look at the behaviour of employee representatives on Norwegian boards, it becomes clear that
although they share legally in the power of the board they
find it very difficult to see how to use that power in ways
that are in accord with the usual board purposes and at
the same time make a direct impact on the working life of
their constituents."

Although we would accept the danger inherent in comparisons between different social systems, the German data
does seem to highlight adequately the difficulties exper-
ienced by the workers in their relationship with the
representative; a lack of contact and a lack of knowledge of
the role appear to be the most common features. A further
problem, evident in the Norwegian experience, is that faced
by the participant who is exposed to conflicting expectations
about the performance of his role. For instance, he may be
convinced both by managerial arguments, which stress the
need for cost reductions and increased efficiency, and his
fellow workers' needs for improved wages and job security.
Both interest groups could expect the employee director to
express their viewpoint and could well attempt to impose
pressures to achieve that end. The Norwegian experience
clearly indicated the difficulties that the worker directors
faced in their attempt to make an impact on the lives of the
ordinary worker.

To summarize, available overseas experience and the
initial evidence for the BSC experiment would seem to
suggest that this type of participation has not succeeded in
making a significantly positive impact on management
decisions, or in conveying a sense of involvement to the
worker. At the same time, the role seems to suffer from
being one of potential conflict.

CONTROL OVER PARTICIPANTS

The relationship between the representative and his constituents is an item of particular relevance to the present
discussion of indirect participation, as well as being an area

of current controversy. It has now become widely accepted that voluntary organizations are generally subject to the administration of the few, with the majority displaying a high level of non-involvement and apathy. Michels (1915) was amongst the first to write about this relationship between mass apathy and internal democracy in working class organizations, and put forward a wide range of possible explanations for what he regarded as an inevitable tendency towards oligarchy in trade unions. Not only did he draw attention to situational exigencies (such as the need for a fighting organization to retain centralized control), to members' apathy, and to members' positive demand for leadership, but Michels also suspected that the leaders reinforced the tendency towards oligarchy. On this point, he wrote:

"In the leader, the consciousness of his personal worth, and of the need which the mass feels for his guidance, combine to induce in his mind a recognition of his own superiority (real or supposed)." (1915, pp 206–207).

In the present context, the principal question relates to the efficacy of the means of control possessed by the ordinary member, which can redress these oligarchic tendencies. It is possible to distinguish between two areas of control:

1 that exercised within the trade union administrative hierarchy, with particular reference to the branch
2 that resulting from shop floor activities and shop steward elections.

All the available evidence would seem to indicate that it is within the workplace that the content and the quality of the relationship between the member and his representative is determined. This has been recognized by the TGWU in particular; as a result the union has encouraged the steward to play a more dominant role, with a possible loss of status and power for the union's full-time officials. However, this trend is by no means accepted by all unions. If they are put into practice, the registration provisions of the Industrial Relations Act 1971 could force trade unions to clarify the relationship between the shop steward and the formal union hierarchy.

The importance of the workplace as the focus of bargaining activities can be explained largely by the meaning attached to trade unionism by the members. The branch, which is generally organized on a geographical and/or occupational basis, can be viewed as a unit for social action possessing a greater ideological content than the mere determination of wages within a particular enterprise. Because of this, for those workers to whom the financial rewards of labour are paramount, limited importance has been attached to branch activities; on the other hand, trade unions in the workplace will have a particular significance as they are often dealing primarily with monetary issues. Attitudes of this nature will be reinforced by the increasing emphasis upon plant bargaining.

Although dealing with a limited and specifically defined group of workers, Goldthorpe *et al* (1968) produced evidence illustrative of the trend to which we have referred. For instance, they quote one typical respondent as saying: "The only aspect of the union I'm interested in is what goes on in this factory" (p 100). Summing up the data collected, it was suggested that the style of unionism exhibited could be most usefully described as "instrumental collectivism – collectivism, that is to say, which is directed to the achievement of individuals' private goals, outside the workplace" (1968, p 106 – see also Goldthorpe and Lockwood, 1963). Such an approach can only be acted out in the context of the workplace.

Evidence is readily available to support the assertion that control is likely to be at its greatest in the workplace. In his detailed study of trade union government and administration, Roberts (1956) found that attendance at branch meetings was generally limited to between three per cent and 15 per cent of members, depending among other things upon the type of labour recruited, and the location of the branch. It was generally assumed that skilled workers displayed a greater propensity to participate in branch affairs. However, in a recent study of shipbuilding workers in Wallsend – traditional occupational groups in what might be considered a traditional working class community, and therefore more likely to place a higher premium on solidarity – Brown and Brannen (1970) found a low participation rate in branch affairs. Only 11 per cent of the members attended union meetings 'always', hardly portraying a very strong commitment to unionism, particularly when it is remembered that a large percentage of those interviewed were craftsmen. Nevertheless, when turning their attention to shopfloor activities, the authors discovered a high level of involvement in union affairs. "Attendance at various workplace union meetings called by shop stewards . . . appears to be nearly 100 per cent and union affairs are discussed with interest when issues involving a particular occupational group arise" (p 78). This implies that control over the shop steward is more likely to be exerted at the place of work through shopfloor meetings and day to day contact. It is not unreasonable to suggest that these informal pressures will be used more fully in times of rapid inflation in an attempt to satisfy the members' demand for wage increases and, in these circumstances, the steward's role can become primarily concerned with reflecting rather than directing opinions. Consistent with this viewpoint, the works managers and personnel officers who formed part of the Government Social Survey sample held the view that trade union members were more militant than their shop stewards. (See also Cousins, 1972). No longer, it seems, is the shop steward able to commit his members to an agreement without detailed consultation. If this is so, it is a sign of the increasing desire for control, and symptomatic of a tendency for indirect areas of participation to become subject to direct scrutiny.

An additional means of control is provided by the system of shop steward election. In the study of the 'affluent' worker already referred to, 83 per cent of the trade unionists in the sample voted regularly at shop steward elections. Goldthorpe *et al*, 1969). This must be contrasted with the

Government Social Survey (1968) sample of shop stewards, of whom only 29 per cent had been opposed in election procedures. This does not necessarily mean that control is not exercised over the shop steward: the constituents might be satisfied with the activities of the steward on their behalf or it may simply reflect a lack of concern. No evidence is available to enable us to form any definitive conclusions.

THE IMPLICATIONS FOR DIRECT PARTICIPATION

In this chapter we have noted the extent to which certain indirect forms of participation enable workers to exert control over various types of decision. Indirect forms of participation are important to our subsequent analysis of direct participation for a number of reasons.

1 Since they have traditionally constituted the dominant form of participation, they represent the main alternative to the direct forms.
2 They have allowed us to illustrate the type of issues which the worker considers to be important. We have noted the tendency to extend collective bargaining and joint regulation at the expense of joint consultation. The latter was criticized for its inability to provide both a platform for discussion of contentious issues and the possibility of joint decision-making. In addition, in our discussion of the relationshop between shop stewards and their constituents, we detected an increasing pressure for workers to exert their control in dealing with matters they deemed important. In other words, it could be argued that the role of shop steward was being changed from that of representative to that of delegate.
3 By highlighting the problems presented to management by the trends in collective bargaining and by the failure of joint consultation as an alternative, they highlight the pressures to seek a different approach. Managers can react in two main ways to this; one is to call for greater formal regulation of the bargaining process; the other is to look

for alternative means whereby they can achieve their objectives and at the same time meet the needs of the workforce. It is in this context that direct participation can be useful, particularly if it helps to turn attention towards those issues which managers define as important or safe. In our discussion of productivity bargaining, we suggested that in certain cases management placed some emphasis upon the increased possibilities for job satisfaction as a result of the proposed changes in job content and working conditions, whereas workers were more concerned with pay and job security. This is illustrative both of the differing definitions attached to participation, and also the potential relationship between direct and indirect participation.

Summary

This chapter has examined the two main forms of indirect control currently found in the United Kingdom, namely collective bargaining and joint consultation, and has also reviewed United Kingdom experience with worker directors. After examining the control offered to the workers' representatives by each type of participation, the relationship between representative and represented was analysed.

Collective bargaining. Because of its concern with pay and conditions of employment, collective bargaining has constituted the most important form of participation. The opportunity for company-based representatives to exert marked control over pay and conditions began to increase only after the mid-1950s. The growth of plant bargaining led to a growth in the number of shop stewards and a challenge to the established frontiers of control. This challenge was most marked in the context of productivity bargaining, which allowed representatives to become concerned with a whole new range of topics. There is evidence of pressure for a further considerable extension of control by workers' representatives although some may prefer to retain a focus on questions of pay, conditions and security.

In contrast, the Industrial Relations Act represents an attempt to limit and regulate the extent of this control.

Joint consultation. This has operated primarily as a means of communication. The content of the communication has often consisted of historical issues or issues of marginal interest to the majority of workers. Because of this, and because it permits the bulk of control to reside with management, it has declined considerably in popularity from its post-war peak. This decline has been accelerated by the growth of plant bargaining and the increased use of supervisors as a channel of communication.

Worker directors. Since 1968, the British Steel Corporation has had a number of worker directors on the board of its main product divisions, though not on its main board. A review of their impact shows that they suffer from problems similar to those of worker directors in other countries, namely difficulties in maintaining sufficient knowledge for the role and a conflict of interest. This suggests that, as representatives of the workforce, their impact has been minimal.

Control over representatives is exerted primarily at the workplace through formal and informal contact with shop stewards and through their election. In recent years there has been a tendency, more particularly in times of crisis such as a threatened closure, to take direct action. It also seems likely that in certain industries increased shop-floor involvement has meant that the shop steward must act as representative rather than delegate.

There is currently considerable pressure from both sides of industry either to limit or extend the topics which constitute issues for collective bargaining. At the same time management is seeking alternative channels for worker interest and involvement; in this context many managers may view the direct forms of participation as distinctly promising.

NOTES

1 We are concentrating in this chapter on those forms of participation currently to be found in the United Kingdom. This means that we shall not be referring in any detail to the European experience with supervisory boards and works councils except in so far as this can be drawn upon to illustrate specific points from the British experience. Furthermore, while we are concerned with existing forms, we acknowledge that despite opposition from important sectors of management and the trade unions, the Government, influenced by a directive from the European Economic Community, may be forced to add to or alter the structure of indirect participation. We would expect that, without the active cooperation and enthusiasm of both sides of industry, the impact of any such changes would be minimal.

2 A unilateral management system of control appears to have been a significant feature of a productivity agreement described by D A Gotting, The Introduction of a Wage Grading and Productivity Plan in a Large Engineering Firm, *British Journal of Industrial Relations*, vol ix, no 3, November 1971, pp 314–329.

CHAPTER THREE

THE CULTURAL AND PSYCHO-LOGICAL DETERMINANTS OF WORK AND WORK BEHAVIOUR

As we have already indicated, the possibility of participation by subordinates has been discussed in a number of different contexts. Our concern centres upon work organizations; it is intended in this chapter to discuss briefly the importance and meaning of work and to develop a theoretical framework for the understanding of reactions to schemes of direct participation.

THE FUNCTIONS OF WORK

In a modern, complex industrial society, to say that work has a particular importance is no more than a truism. Such is its importance that Sofer (1970), for instance, has been able to list nine main functions that can be attached to work roles:

1 to provide economic returns that are a means to other ends
2 to provide the person with opportunities to relate himself to society
3 to enable the person to sustain status and self-respect
4 to provide opportunities for interaction with others
5 to contribute to personal identity
6 to structure the passage of time
7 to help ward off distressing thoughts and feelings
8 to provide scope for personal achievement
9 to test and affirm personal competence.

Of these, four appear to have particular significance.

First, in all societies, some form of work activity is an essential aid to existence for an overwhelming majority of the population. Even if the fisherman and hunter of more primitive societies have been replaced by workers in the highly developed technologies of our own time, work still retains its basic economic significance for all groups. While the purpose of work may have changed from the need to survive to the need to satisfy high level patterns of consumption, the primary function of work for many people continues to be partly instrumental.

Secondly, work assumes an additional significance in so far as it affords status. This leads to the ranking of occupations in a prestige hierarchy. The relevance of the status function is readily noticeable in studies of the unemployed (see for instance Bakke, 1933).

Thirdly, the development of industrial technologies has created a constraint upon an individual. No longer is time free; instead it is largely structured to serve the ends of production. The discipline provided by industry has been noted in the context of developing countries as well as during the industrial revolution in Britain. On this point, Thompson (1967) comments: "The first generation were taught by the masters the importance of time. The second generation founded their short-time committees in the ten-hour movement; the third generation struck for overtime or time and a half. They had captured the categories of their employers and learned to fight back within them. They had learnt their lesson that time is money, only too well". The constraint of work would seem to extend beyond the immediate work situation; studies of non-work behaviour suggest a relationship between type of leisure activities and the nature of work. (Parker, 1965, 1971; Brown *et al*, 1972).

Finally, given the central relevance of work as a life activity, it is argued by many not only that work can provide opportunities for achievement and growth but also that it should offer such opportunities. As we shall see, this approach constitutes a central theme of those who advocate greater control over task performance.

In the general literature on work it is possible to differentiate two approaches. First, there are those writers who generally subscribe to some idealistic image of work, as a creative, satisfying activity in its own right, immune from the discipline of capital, technology and time. Marx, for instance, in his well-known comments on communism and the abolition of the division of labour, envisaged a context in which work would not be alienated labour but a pursuit involving freedom of choice and action; man would be enabled to achieve his real self through the fulfilment provided by work. "In a communist society, where nobody has an exclusive sphere of activity, but each can be accomplished in any branch he wishes, society regulates the general production and thus makes it possible for one to do one thing today, and another tomorrow, to hunt in the morning, fish in the afternoon, rear cattle in the evening, criticize after dinner, just as I have a mind, without ever becoming hunter, fisherman, shepherd or critic" (Marx and Engels, 1965 pp 44-45).

On a distinctly less utopian level, but still seeing work as an end in itself, Mills (1957) has developed an ideal typical formulation of non-alienated labour, in the form of craftsmanship. The main features of this form of work concern the individual's ability to gain satisfaction from and control over the performance of tasks. Unlike alienated labour, there will be no sharp distinction between work and non-work, as the individual will bring to his leisure activities the values and qualities developed during his working time.* The concept of craftsmanship as the ideal type of work has influenced a number of empirical studies of job satisfaction. Amongst Blauner's (1960) samples of workers, for instance, his group of craft workers was found to be the least alienated. He postulated an inverted U-shaped curve to demonstrate the relationship between type of technology

---

* This integration of work and non-work has been most noted in studies of professional groups (see eg Parker, 1971).

and the level of alienation. As technological systems advanced from craft to continuous process, alienation would increase and then decrease again; Blauner felt that continuous process technologies could offer opportunities for satisfaction almost as significant as those found in craft production. Blauner's approach can be criticized on a number of grounds (see, for instance, Eldridge, 1971) not least because he fails to distinguish between structural variables and feeling states. Although the structure of industry might appear to be such as to maximize feelings of alienation, the worker's model of a non-alienated state is likely to be constrained by his view of existing social reality.

The possibilities of achieving the utopian dream of liberated work have been diminished from one viewpoint by the processes and pressures of industrialization, and from another by the nature and forces of capitalism. In his discussion of surplus value and capital accumulation, Marx dealt with the nature of work under capitalism. All attempts to increase 'the productiveness of work' were seen as being at the expense of the worker. Accumulated capital will be directed towards increasing the surplus value of each individual worker, a process whose inevitable outcome will be the increased misery of every worker.

Many writers have noted an evolutionary trend among industrial societies towards a greater degree of similarity; a similarity characterized by a complex and highly developed division of labour, and an increasing consensus and coherence. They have failed to discuss the possibility of alienations resulting from division of labour (see, for instance, Kerr *et al*, 1964). These views can be contrasted with those of Marcuse (1964), who sees all forms of advanced technology societies as totalitarian, typified by a lack of freedom and reason. Nevertheless, both types of analysis can be criticized for viewing behaviour as being largely technologically determined; a preferable view would not deny the importance of technology for the social division of labour, but would regard it as incorrect to view man as being unable to select between alternative courses of action.

Indeed, the strategies for increasing job satisfaction discussed in the subsequent chapters assume a choice within the constraints set by technology.

In contrast to those who stress that work should be an end in itself, the second group of writers see work more as a means to an end. In *The Protestant Ethic and the Spirit of Capitalism*, Weber (1930) discussed the relevance of Calvinist and Lutheran religious reforms to the rise of capitalism. Rational work activity was considered a pursuit in God's glory and, as such, contained its own significance. Work therefore had little need to possess intrinsic meaning as the concept of duty assumed overriding importance. Dull and monotonous work would be accepted; change would be tolerable. From this base, the search for rationality in production methods had and would develop its own dynamic to such an extent, Weber argued, that the economic and technological system of machine production would determine the lives of all individuals. A system of domination had emerged; as duty gave way to domination, so the spirit of asceticism was subordinated to the goal of consumption. "Material goods have gained an increasing and finally an inexorable power over the lives of men as at no previous period in history" (1930, p 181). It is impossible to deny the importance of consumption in our society (see D Bell, 1961, for a discussion of work and the cult of efficiency). Political parties are judged upon their ability to stimulate growth while the social costs of such policies in relation to employment and job content are largely ignored. Indeed, it is interesting to compare the publicity and attention given to environmental problems outside the work organization with the important question of the nature of work within the context of particular working conditions. Only belatedly has the 'quality of working life' become an issue for general discussion.

Seen as a means, work can serve different but compatible ends. Task content can be subordinated to rational efficiency; in turn, efficiency can stimulate and satisfy new levels of consumption. It would appear that at the present time the workers have become consumer-oriented and, as such, have accepted the dominant aims of capitalism. Indeed, modern capitalism would appear to be increasingly dependent upon the growth of consumption, although particular sectional interests must be persuaded not to maximize their own ability to consume, to avoid dysfunctional consequences such as inflation. It is within this process of enhancing one's ability to consume that many writers have detected the inherent instability of capitalism; if the desire for material wants is satiated, the workers' instrumental collectivism might be channelled towards challenging the existing order of control (Mallet, 1963; Anderson, 1968). At present, there is sufficient evidence that the worker is primarily concerned with maximizing satisfaction as a consumer. The studies by Goldthorpe *et al* (1968) and Ingham (1970) are indicative of the contexts in which workers are prepared to accept high wages, and the ability to satisfy material objectives, at the cost of tedious and dissatisfying work.

Our discussion in the subsequent chapters will focus upon strategies that aim to invest work with intrinsic meaning. If we accept the primacy of the consumption ethic, it becomes apparent that such approaches are only acceptable in so far as they help to achieve growth. Fox (1971, p 12) makes a similar point: "The advocacy of self actualization as the reference point by which work should be judged is vitiated unless it comes to grips with the role of work in serving purely economic or consumer values. . . . Men assess work in terms of what it does *for* them, as well as what it does *to* them". Whilst some industrial psychologists might find sufficient justification for their work in the increased job satisfaction of the individual worker, society might judge their work in relation to efficiency and consumption.

PARTICIPATION AND WORK

Schemes of direct participation which are based upon aims of increasing both job satisfaction and organizational effectiveness consider work to be both an end in itself and a means to an end. The ideas based upon Maslow's (1943) hierarchy of needs (for a discussion of this see the last section of this chapter) are concerned with providing opportunities for the satisfaction of higher level needs of the individual, such as growth and achievement. The application of Maslow's ideas to industry is based on the assumption that the worker who has the opportunity to satisfy his need for self-actualization will contribute more effectively to the organization. To this extent, the theorists of direct participation can be distinguished from those writers who are concerned about work *per se* in so far as, whilst the initial emphasis is placed upon the individual, the overriding practical objective appears to be a more efficient and effective organization. Given the organizationally based orientations of managers, it is highly likely that work, and by implication schemes of participation, will be valued in relation to this contribution towards the attainment of organizational objectives. This would indicate that neither direct nor indirect schemes of participation will be precluded, although the management literature displays a distinct bias towards the former (see chapter 4).

In chapter 1, four main objectives of participation were outlined. Two of these would appear to be of particular significance for managers, namely to improve both productivity and industrial relations.

1 *Participation as a means of improving productivity*

It is hoped that, by giving the workforce more freedom to pursue desirable outcomes, they will at the same time raise production levels (production must be used in its widest sense to include all goods and services). Walker (1970) has given seven reasons why this might happen:

    workers have ideas which might be useful
    effective upward communications will improve top level
    decision-making
    workers will more readily accept decisions in which they
    participate

workers will work harder if they share in decisions affecting them

workers will work more intelligently if they know what is going on and why and they know they can influence this

participation will improve teamwork and reduce conflict

participation will act as a spur to management efficiency.

These reasons fail to make explicit the argument which is often applied to productivity bargaining, but which is equally relevant here, that productivity will be improved by allowing management and the workforce to pursue separate but not incompatible goals. This is generally applied to the instrumental rewards of participation such as giving the worker control to earn more money if, at some time, he produces more. In Fox's terminology, the image of the economic organization is largely unitary or what in the Introduction, we have called integrative.

2 *Participation as a means of improving industrial relations*

A breakdown in industrial relations can sometimes be a stimulus to the introduction of productivity bargaining or worker participation. Since such breakdowns are seen as being very costly, the improvement of industrial relations and the promotion of calm and peaceful relations can be a specific objective. One approach to industrial conflict has seen it as a reaction to overpowering managerial controls. Referring to Argyris' (1957, 1964) argument that the response to the frustration engendered by these controls is regressive behaviour which manifests itself in conflict behaviour, it is suggested that by giving the workforce more control over its environment, a major cause of frustration would be removed. This in turn might lead to more mature behaviour and in particular more open communications. Yet again, the control exerted by the worker will be contained within a framework determined by management and thereby contributing towards managerial objectives.

MOTIVATIONAL PERSPECTIVES IN DIRECT PARTICIPATION

To provide a full understanding of the nature of direct participation, it is essential to construct a model to explain why workers should want to participate, and why they should favour particular forms of participation. Work motivation is a topic which has been extensively researched, but whose complexity has allowed only limited progress towards a detailed understanding. In the remainder of this chapter, we will describe and develop one approach to the study of motivation and adapt it to fit in with the discussion of direct forms of participation. In other words, the preceding abstract discussion of work will be placed in a motivation model.

The expectancy model

Broadly speaking, it is possible to distinguish two basic approaches to the study of motivation in the context of work. First, there are what can be termed content models: these are concerned with describing the nature of the various needs within an individual which can 'motivate' him to behave in a certain way. They implicitly accept the principle of homeostasis* and the existence of physiological and psychological disequilibrium. Behaviour is motivated by the desire to restore equilibrium by satisfying the need. Thus the hungry man seeks food and the lonely man seeks company.

Secondly, there are process models which are more concerned to explain the nature of motivated behaviour and to understand why and under what conditions a man will act in a certain way. The one which has attracted most attention is the expectancy-instrumentality-valence theory, or, as it is more simply called, expectancy theory. This was initially developed by Tolman (1932) and Lewin (1938), and was first applied to industry by Vroom (1964). Expectancy

---

* Homeostasis is a physiological term which refers to the tendency of the human body to compensate for and adjust to changes in the external environment.

theory as described by Porter and Lawler (1968) can be described diagrammatically (see Figure 2).

Motivated behaviour, or effort, is dependent upon three conditions. The first, referred to as Type I Expectancy, is the subjective belief on the part of an individual that by exerting effort he will be able to accomplish a given task. The second condition, referred to as Type II Expectancy, is the subjective belief that by successfully accomplishing the task he will obtain the reward he seeks. Both these types of expectancy will be influenced by the individual's perception of the task and of his own skill, and also by his previous experience of similar situations. The third condition is that the individual must perceive that there are attractive rewards available to him if he successfully accomplishes the task. This is a complex issue which we discuss more fully a little later; for the present, it is fairly clear that if the individual is not attracted by the available rewards he will

Figure 2

The Porter-Lawler Expectancy Model

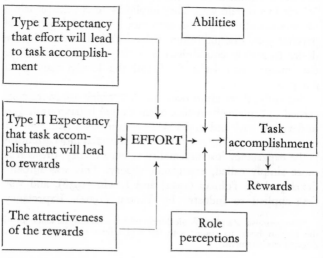

be less likely to exert effort. These three conditions are multiplicative to the extent that the absence of any one of them is likely severely to limit the amount of motivated behaviour. But given the existence of all three types of expectancy, effort is likely to result.

The relationship between effort and successful performance in the form of task accomplishment is mediated by a number of factors. Two of the most important are the influence of an individual's ability and the accuracy with which he has understood the total situation and knows how to direct his effort. Someone who is not competent to utilize his effort or someone who has failed to grasp the situation, particularly in relation to Type I Expectancy (that effort directed in a certain way will lead to task accomplishment) is unlikely to accomplish his task successfully.

The expectancy model is not without critics. The main criticism is that it is too rational. It implies that people look at the relevant factors, weigh them up and then arrive at the best decision. This criticism is not entirely valid in that the emphasis on expectancy implies that it is the subjective perception of the situation that counts, and at any one time irrational factors may colour the perception. A closely related criticism is that motivation can be most clearly observed during change or choice situations; at such times emotion can have a strong influence on behaviour. It is argued that the theory has not overtly considered the role of emotion. This criticism is valid only where emotional factors may not have been taken fully into account when attempting to measure an individual's perceptions and determine the attractiveness of certain rewards. The same criticism can be levelled against every other theory of motivation, with the possible exception of those with a psychoanalytic basis. It is important not to over-rate the role of emotion. For the majority of employees, there is no reason to suppose that emotional considerations vary so dramatically as to obviate the value of measures of expectancy and valence.

On the credit side, expectancy theory has the advantages

of focusing on the reasons for behaviour; it points to certain measurable items and is useful in that it enables predictions to be made. Furthermore, it fits in neatly with our control framework for participation. It will, therefore, be used in our subsequent analysis. Before going further, it is necessary to say something about what constitute attractive rewards.

DETERMINANTS OF ATTRACTIVE REWARDS

The expectancy model predicts that, given control over task accomplishment and the ability to earn rewards and subject to suitably attractive rewards, motivated behaviour will result. We know that people restrict output despite the great attraction of potentially higher earnings. We therefore need to know rather more about costs as well as rewards. In many cases restriction of output occurs because social pressures or fears of redundancy outweigh what may initially appear to be the major reward of money. To be useful, the model must therefore offer some sort of priorities among the possible rewards and it must distinguish between the rewards and the costs of exerting effort. Taking this second point first, the model must be adapted slightly to stipulate that effort will be contingent upon Types I and II, expectancy and the attractiveness of the rewards, taking into account the costs of attaining them.

A number of theories have attempted to outline the most important rewards. Only two offer anything approaching a set of priorities. One of these is Herzberg's (1959, 1966) two-factor theory (for a full discussion see chapter 7) which distinguishes between extrinsic and intrinsic job factors and argues that the intrinsic factors alone are positive motivators. In developing their version of the expectancy model, Porter and Lawler (1968) cited this as the main distinction between types of reward. Briefly, extrinsic factors are those which are irrelevent to the job content and include security, interpersonal relations and company policy. In contrast, intrinsic factors are closely associated with the job content and include scope for achievement, responsibility and personal development.

The second and more sophisticated approach is offered by Maslow (1943). He has argued that needs can be ordered in a hierarchy of priority. At the bottom of the hierarchy are physiological needs which have first priority. These are followed by the need for security and safety and then the need for love and affection. Moving towards the top of the hierarchy, esteem needs come next and include needs for achievement, autonomy and recognition; finally, there is the need for self-actualization or self-fulfilment. Starting from the bottom of the hierarchy, a need operates as a motivator until that need has been satisfied; but once it has been satisfied it ceases to motivate behaviour and the next level becomes the most significant. This is essentially a content theory but it can be contained with the process-type expectancy theory. From a practical point of view, the implication is that once the critical level of motivation has been determined, the appropriate motivators can be provided.

Maslow's model provides a useful framework for looking at alternative rewards but is no real substitute for empirical data. It has a number of serious weaknesses particularly when it is applied to industry. One of the most interesting criticisms comes from Maslow himself in his notes on *Eupsychian Management* (1965); he wrote (p 55) that "a good deal of the evidence upon which he (McGregor) bases his conclusions comes from my researches and my papers on motivation, self-actualization etc. But I of all people should know just how shaky this foundation is as a final foundation. My work on motivation comes from the clinic, from a study of neurotic people. The carry over of this theory to the industrial situation has some support from industrial studies, but certainly I would like to see a lot more studies of this kind before feeling finally convinced that this carry-over from the study of neurosis to the study of labour in factories is legitimate".

Probably the major study of the relevance of Maslow's

ideas to industry was conducted by Porter (1961, 1962, 1963) who concluded that the differences in the importance attached to various needs by managers of different levels could be interpreted in terms of Maslow's theory. Many other studies have produced findings which fit Maslow's hierarchy but none of them test it in a satisfactory way. In the industrial context it is hard to see how it can be realistically tested, without conducting what would almost certainly be a socially unacceptable type of experiment. In other words, it remains descriptive rather than predictive for all practical purposes.

Another difficulty with Maslow's hierarchy, which is particularly relevant to our studies of participation, is the role of money. This is usually classified alongside physiological needs at the bottom of the hierarchy. Yet this seems to be totally misleading since money can, for some people at least, open the door to the satisfaction of a wide variety of needs at all levels of the hierarchy. With some people it might almost be appropriate to perceive money as a general reinforcer.

A further criticism, not so much of Maslow's ideas as of the way in which they have been used, is that they may be satisfied at work or elsewhere. A number of writers concerned with motivation in industry have adopted a closed-system approach and assumed that all but the basic needs may most usefully be satisfied in the work-context. Once again this flies in the face of a considerable amount of empirical data.

The expectancy model does not make any general statement about reward priorities or attempt a theoretical explanation of why certain rewards should prove attractive. Indeed, this is a valid criticism of the approach. Instead it relies upon the collection of empirical evidence and implicitly accepts the potential existence of wide differences for personal or situational reasons.

In subsequent chapters, we will examine the priorities given to various rewards by different groups of workers. The method of gathering the data – by questionnaire – may not be altogether satisfactory, but the underlying approach, emphasizing an action frame of reference, seems more sensible than accepting the assumptions of existing alternative models. This recognizes the complexity of the situation and accepts that a variety of factors can influence needs and the perception of what constitutes desirable rewards. However, one can expect to find some common elements among people who work or live in close proximity.

Summary

This chapter has examined the purposes of work and presented a motivational model for the analysis of participation. Since opinions about the functions of work are likely to influence attitudes towards participation, they are of some importance. Apart from its purely instrumental function and its role in providing status and patterning our lives, it could be argued that work should provide scope for achievement, autonomy and self-expression. This would be reflected in demands for an extension of direct participation and such an assumption underlies the writing of those, such as Marx and Blauner who view work in terms of alienation and control. In contrast there are others, such as Weber, who have highlighted a tradition which considers work more as a means to an end. Certainly it seems likely that managers will support a viewpoint and a strategy which is likely to lead to increased productivity and improved industrial relations.

To understand what workers want out of work, and hence help to explain how they are likely to react to various types of participation, an expectancy theory of motivation has been presented. This suggests that motivated behaviour, or effort, is most likely to occur when there is a perceived relationship between effort and performance and between performance and reward, given the existence of attractive rewards. Whether or not this effort results in effective performance will depend upon the individual's ability and the accuracy with which he has understood his role. Although not without its weaknesses, this approach provides useful guidelines for our subsequent analysis of direct forms of participation. It does beg the question of what constitute attractive rewards; while the theories of Herzberg (1966) and more particularly Maslow (1943) can provide some useful guidelines to this, they are no substitute for empirical data.

CHAPTER FOUR

MANAGEMENT AND PARTICIPATION

Drucker (1954) has argued that management is, amongst other things, "a system of values and beliefs". Knowles and Saxberg (1967) make the issue even broader by claiming that "the quality of human relations in any organization . . . reflects first of all its members', and particularly its leaders' views of the essential character of humanity itself" (1967, p 178). They go on to say that these values are reflected in the way social relations are structured, in the system of rewards and punishments, in the character of the communication processes and in the system of social control. In other words, ideology will influence behaviour.

An increasingly orthodox viewpoint has argued that the values and processes of management have undergone significant changes as a result of the development of a capitalism which is no longer solely concerned with profit maximization. This view represents the optimistic variant of the thesis dealing with the divorce between ownership and control in industry, and is typified by a particular comment from Crossland (1962) who asserts that economic power is now exercised in a significantly more responsible manner. It is not our concern to discuss this particular thesis in detail, but rather to see whether an increased responsibility is reflected in management's thinking on participation.

In this chapter, two methods of analysis and argument will be used: first, we shall discuss the literature dealing with management's views on participation and secondly, almost in contrast, we shall analyse questionnaire responses from a sample of managers. This new empirical data is a limited attempt to fill the significant vacuum left by the literature; we recognize that the vast majority of managers,

63

including those in our sample, are unconscious thinkers in that they rarely put down on paper their own views on the management process. But, those who do publicize their thoughts are seen by Child (1969) as the "active members of what is sometimes called the British management movement" (p 23). Any review must almost inevitably concentrate upon the attitudes and beliefs of this second group; however, Child (1969) admitted that these managers were sometimes out of touch with the thinking of the majority of practising managers, so some counterbalance is desirable.

THE MANAGEMENT LITERATURE AND PARTICIPATION

Before turning to the relevant literature, it is worth considering why individual managers feel that it is necessary or desirable to present their ideas on how best to manage their human resources. Child (1969) has suggested a useful framework by drawing a distinction between the technical and 'legitimatory' functions of such ideas. The writing which presents management ideas is technical in so far as it tells management how to manage and it is 'legitimatory' in so far as it helps management to justify why it has the right to manage. Participation offers a relevant illustration of these functions: writing on participation can be seen as technical because it creates a body of knowledge and theory whose purpose it is to improve the utilization of the economic and human resources of the enterprise. It is argued, for instance, that participation can be instrumental in achieving greater worker cooperation and efficiency, despite the conflicting demands and pressures of new and changing technologies. In terms of legitimacy, participation is advanced as a technique which allows economic power to be exercised by management for the good of all and with the acceptance of all the workers. This emphasis upon the technical and legitimatory functions of managerial literature will be highlighted in the subsequent discussion of participation.

Management thinking has a particular significance in relation to participation. Over the years, most of the pressure to extend indirect forms of participation has come from the workers. In contrast, management itself has usually taken the initiative in advocating the various forms of direct participation.[1] This reflects a potential contradiction in management's thinking: while generally seeking to retain control over the workforce and over decision-making, management at the same time proposes to give the workers the control implied by direct participation. The problems this presents for management will clearly vary according to the amount of control involved and attempts to deal with this issue are reflected in much of the management writing.

THE MAJOR MANAGERIAL PERSPECTIVES ON PARTICIPATION

It is widely accepted that there are three, possibly four, perspectives which reflect management's attitude towards its human resources. In the literature they are viewed as being sequential in that one tends to follow from the other: whilst this may be true of their emergence, it does not follow that the arrival of a new approach heralded the demise of the old. Nevertheless, whilst the technical application of each perspective might not be time-constrained, the emergence of a particular perspective and its legitimatory function would appear to be closely related. For instance, the emergence of what we shall call the 'social man' perspective can be set against a background of strongly voiced criticisms of the ability and the right of the managerial élite to control economic and human resources. Equally, the concept of intrinsically motivated man can be seen in the light of the development of a new, and different, order of problems for management, arising from the pace and nature of technological change. It is not surprising that the resulting participative techniques are task-centred and, as such, are in line with the current debate on job satisfaction and alienation.

65

The three major perspectives, if taken to their logical extremes, all allow for some form of direct participation. The first, that of economic man, based on the school of scientific management, assumes the development of motivation through a system of financial rewards and punishments. By allowing the worker some freedom to decide the rate at which he wants to work, it also allows him the control to influence production through restrictive practices or even unofficial strikes. The second major perspective, that of social man, swung away from the emphasis on the individual and financial incentives and concentrated instead on the role of the work group. This facilitated the development of participative styles of leadership, a more open communication system and group involvement in decision-making. Extending this further, the perspective of the intrinsically motivated man, the third major perspective, was based on a hierarchy of human needs and implied that industrial man had reached a level in this hierarchy where he would respond to the opportunity for responsibility, recognition, achievement and growth. This led to the overlapping techniques of job enrichment and work structuring. Suggestion schemes can be seen as logically related to this perspective although they have a much longer history in industry.

It is possible to distinguish a fourth perspective, although it may be more correct to regard it as an amalgam of the previous three. Schein (1965) describes it as the acceptance of a complex man. Child (1969) sees it as the breakdown of a clear line in British management thought. This is the pragmatic approach adopted by those who argue that there is no one correct strategy and that industrial motivation and control depend on a great many complex and inter-related factors. Only by understanding which of these various factors are in operation in a particular environment is it possible to begin to understand how best to use the human resources. Clearly this approach will not advocate any particular form of participation, but it shows how the previous three perspectives can become merged.

ECONOMIC MAN

The concept of economic man is usually traced back to the writings of F W Taylor (1947) and the school of scientific management. Although similar themes had been developed by earlier writers, Taylor attracted more attention because his work appeared at a time when management was under pressure from the increasingly powerful union movement. The *laissez faire* movement in Britain and the defenders of the 'open shop' in America welcomed his writings from an ideological viewpoint because he apparently disclaimed the need for unions to exist. However, it is for his technical contribution, as the father of work-study, that Taylor is perhaps chiefly remembered. His approach held a number of motivational assumptions which had and still have a strong appeal to management. These assumptions crystalize the feelings of many managers about how to control the workforce; not only have they been influential but they also have clear implications for both direct and indirect forms of participation.

Taylor's aim was to systematize the work process by determining standard times for each operation. He used time and motion study to determine what constituted a 'fair day's work' for what he called 'a first class man'. The scientific measurement of a fair day's work was one critical part of his system; the other was to set an appropriate rate of pay and establish a piecework system. It was expected that the use of an incentive payment scheme would raise productivity. This reflected the underlying assumption that money was the key motivator, although Taylor related this to what he felt was the worker's strong competitive instinct to do well. At the same time, he upheld some of the beliefs inherent in the Protestant ethic by arguing that the best type of worker will be docile, ready to accept management changes and will not carp at dull, heavy or monotonous work.

As a means of retaining management control over the workforce, scientific management was seen to have a number of merits. Furthermore, Taylor managed to produce some dramatic improvements in performance by using his techniques; there is little doubt that he and some of his early followers made a significant contribution to the technical efficiency of many organizations. It was often easy to convince managers that economic motives had a central role in the lives of workers since it fitted in with their own beliefs and was often supported by their observation experience.

The implication of effort-related reward in any dynamic system – and Taylor accepted that industry must be viewed as dynamic – is that there will be a strain on the effort-bargain. Although this can arise from a questioning of the legitimacy of the work-measurement techniques, it is equally likely to arise as a result of pressures outside the work environment, such as inflation, inter-industrial comparisons and a rise in the general standard of living. Where a variety of piece-rates exists, there is scope for long-term conflict and, by implication, the freedom provided by the payment system gives the worker enough control to be able to force management to bargain with him. This unintended consequence of the incentive scheme was not foreseen by Taylor. He felt that any low output worker should be punished and he introduced a harsh system to do so. But the more acceptable system introduced by Gantt (1919), coupled with the growing power of the unions, which enabled them to fix minimum levels of pay in a number of instances, ruled this out. In any case Taylor did not expect that his system would lead to greater conflict: he adopted a functionalist, almost idealistic approach and argued that, since his scientific management ensured that everyone was treated fairly, there was no real need to bargain with unions. Instead, in a spirit of mutual cooperation, both management and worker would strive to increase the general wealth. This implied that the worker would want to participate in such a scheme. A number of subsequent writers on scientific management have rather neglected this aspect of Taylor's ideas; they have tended instead to reflect the feelings of some of those managers who tried to put his ideas into practice but who could not agree with him that authoritarian management was unnecessary.

What Taylor advocated, and the assumptions of Taylorism as it was (and still is) practised are rather different. It was adapted both to the realities of the industrial situation and to the needs of managers who used it. Perhaps the best known exposition of these assumptions is to be found in the writings of McGregor (1960). He described Theory X as "a theory which materially influences managerial strategy in a wide sector of American industry today" (1960, p 35). It rests, so he claimed, upon three major assumptions:

1 The average human being has an inherent dislike of work and will avoid it if he can.
2 Because of this human characteristic of dislike of work, most people must be coerced, controlled, directed and threatened with punishment to get them to put forth adequate effort towards the achievement of organizational objectives.
3 The average human being prefers to be directed, wishes to avoid responsibility, has relatively little ambition and wants security above all.

Schein (1965) has added some further assumptions to this list which serve to clarify the management needs which are met by this approach:

1 Man is primarily motivated by economic incentives.
2 Economic incentives are under the control of the organization; so man is essentially passive and can be manipulated, motivated and controlled by the organization.
3 Man's feelings are essentially irrational and must be prevented from interfering with his rational calculation of self-interest.
4 Organizations can and must be designed to neutralize and control man's feelings and his unpredictable traits.

One further assumption, which Schein related to Theory X, but which emerges from these four points is that there are basically two types of men; those born to labour and those born to manage. Although this contradicts the American ethic, it follows on logically from the other assumptions and can be easily assimilated into the manager's approach.

In analysing the functions of ideology, Bendix (1956) has argued the case for adopting an historical approach. It is also useful, as Child (1969) indicated, to examine the factors at play at the time of the emergence of an ideology. We have already stated that Taylorism emerged at a time when managerial authority in America and Britain was, for the first time, being seriously challenged by organized groups of workers. It provided both a justification for the retention of management control and a set of techniques whereby this was made possible. However, most managers either only accepted Taylor's ideas in part or used them to their own ends and this has led to the distortions of his work that appear in the summaries provided by McGregor and Schein. Bendix (1956) has suggested that "the social philosophy rather than the techniques of scientific management became a part of prevailing managerial ideology. Some managers still saw ownership or their own 'excellence' as the justification for their control and resented the intrusion of scientific standards. Others saw incentives as a useful means of manipulation and control but were not prepared to undertake the preliminary 'scientific' work that was a necessary basis to any such scheme. The use of scientific standards to eliminate the need for bargaining does not seem to have been used to prevent the spread of union power. Instead, managers preferred to tighten their controls, particularly through the use of incentive schemes and, particularly after 1918, to improve working conditions and use consultative machinery as a talking shop with the unions" (1956, p 281).

Few managers, until recently, have seen the contradictions inherent in this whole approach.[2] On the one hand it supports the retention of tight managerial control through the manipulation of financial incentives. On the other it

70

supports the idea that a worker, given the freedom of choice, will decide to work harder if by so doing he can obtain financial reward. The basis of control, the financial incentive, also provides the worker with the freedom to decide how he will act. Since there are few working environments in which Taylor's ideal scheme of tight control and strict sanctions are or can be put into practice, the worker is in a position to exert his own means of control by not responding to the incentive and thereby restricting or at least not optimizing output. The conflicts which are often inherent in incentive payment schemes can easily lead to more extreme forms of behaviour such as withdrawal of labour, either as a group, or individually through absenteeism or resignation. These various forms of worker control are unexpected consequences of the approach and can be classed as direct forms of participation.[3]

This sort of behaviour on the part of the worker only serves to confirm the belief of some managers that workers are illogical. On the other hand Whyte (1955), Roy (1952) and others have shown that workers have what, from their own point of view is a logical reason for their behaviour; in fact they partly confirm the tenet that man is primarily motivated by economic incentives and that this is so, even when he is restricting output. Schein (1965) has suggested that the economic man approach is inevitably self-fulfilling and that this largely accounts for its wide acceptance today. Some psychologists, usually associated with the intrinsically-motivated man perspective, argue that if you treat workers like children they will behave like children. If you deny them the opportunity for self-expression, they become hostile and indifferent. Their regressive behaviour takes the form of aggression and focuses on money as the most contentious and obvious issue.

We would offer a rather different interpretation. The economic man perspective demonstrates that where the worker attaches sufficient value or importance to the outcomes and rewards, he will discover a means of exerting control. If he perceives a significantly large disparity in the

71

effort-bargain, he will exert his control, through restriction of output or through other means to put this right. Where there is no disparity or a positive disparity,[4] the worker will use his control to respond positively to the financial incentive.[5] The extent to which the concept of economic man is accepted among current managers is assessed at the end of this chapter. Chapter 5 discusses in some detail the effectiveness of both incentive payment schemes and workers' attempts to control the effort-bargain. This control, where it is not organized through any process of negotiation, is defined as a form of direct participation.

THE HUMAN RELATIONS SCHOOL

Tillet, Kempner and Wills (1970) have suggested that human relations or, as they prefer to call it, the criterion of cooperation "is more a point of view than an operational concept" (p 245). Furthermore, "what is termed 'cooperation' from the standpoint of the organization is, in fact, 'participation' from the viewpoint of the employees" (1970, p 245). It would seem, therefore, to constitute a management perspective which has implications for worker participation.

Child (1969) points out that management thinkers in Britain were beginning to evolve human relations concepts soon after the first world war but that it was not until after the second world war that they reached a wide management audience. Bendix (1956) reports a parallel initial development in the United States, although there the ideas reached and influenced large numbers of managers in the 1920s and 1930s. The work of Mayo (1933) and his associates at the Hawthorne Plant (Roethlisberger and Dickson, 1939) did not therefore initiate the human relations movement but served rather to crystallize and lend scientific support to it. However, for many managers and social scientists, the Hawthorne studies represent a turning point in the development of ideas about man-management.

When the investigation was started in 1924, it initially

reflected the current thinking, namely that low productivity must be caused either by faults in the incentive payment system or by some aspect of the working conditions. As the programme continued over a number of years it became apparent that other factors were influencing production levels. In particular the experiment in the relay assembly test room and the investigation in the bank wiring observation room were interpreted to support the argument that social factors were all-important.

It was apparent that many workers were not responding primarily to the managerial controls which operated through the formal organizational structure and through the incentive payment schemes. Instead, production was influenced by pressures exerted by the social group. However, it was claimed that the appropriate management strategies could ensure that these group pressures could operate in management's favour.

The kind of strategies which management were required to adopt were fairly clearly defined. First of all the ineffectiveness of the formal systems of control must be recognized and instead the informal social system must be accepted and used. Following this, management must strive to get the social group to support rather than oppose organizational objectives. This could be done first through an effective two-way system of communication. The feelings and desires of the workers were to be taken into account; this called for a person-centred, considerate style of supervision and the provision of social and welfare facilities. This led to the concept of the organizational team in which everyone was striving towards the same goal.

Despite the apparent contrast between the human relations movement and scientific management, the underlying assumptions are not necessarily incompatible. In their different ways, both reflect a solidary approach which emphasizes that the interests of management and worker are basically the same and there are no rational grounds for conflict. On the one hand, the causes of conflict, and hence by implication the need for unions, are eliminated by the application of incontestable scientific principles; on the other, conflict is unnecessary where there is commitment to common goals and an effective communications system whereby these goals can be transmitted, assimilated and accepted. Neither need the contrast in emphasis upon economic or social incentives present a contradiction to the manager who believes that the worker is both economically motivated and illogical. In America at least, management did not see worker participation as a relevant factor in the human relations movement. As Bendix (1956) comments: "In this assessment of the managers of industry there was as before a notable emphasis on the gulf which divides them from the common labourer. Nothing but ruin would result if managerial tasks were undertaken by the average worker" (1956, p 283).

In Britain the situation was rather different. Human relations concepts were welcomed by many managers partly as an answer to a number of technical problems but more particularly as a defence against assaults on their legitimacy. A few organizations had used them after 1918 in an attempt to lessen the management-worker crises occurring at the time. More significantly, surveys during the second world war had highlighted the incompetence and ignorance of many managers at a time when they claimed that their authority was justified by their technical competence. Furthermore, the joint production committees, on which both management and workers were represented, had in many cases been an undoubted success and demonstrated the important contribution that workers could make towards solving management problems. The pressures for change and for a new pattern of relationships in industry were reflected in the sweeping election victory of the Labour Party which had campaigned strongly for nationalization.

In response, many managers turned to the human relations concept, which could be presented as the means of developing a special new relationship between management and worker. Great emphasis was placed both upon communications and upon the idea of the team: communi-

74

cations, however, were the cornerstone upon which human relations were built. The communications system was critical because it was used to explain the objectives of management to the worker and to win his acceptance. It was also used to gauge the response of the workers and to anticipate any 'emotional' or 'irrational' actions. The channels of communication were therefore those which management felt were most effective. For some this meant the adaptation of joint production committees into the postwar process of joint consultation. But an increasing number of managers saw dangers here and instead put the emphasis on the formal hierarchical system as the means of communication. The main danger was the growth of a powerful shop-floor organization which could control and influence the flow of information between management and the rest of the workers. It was far safer if management's own representative was responsible for communications. In this way a great deal of pressure was put on the foreman whose job was described by J A C Brown (1954, p 104) as "not only one of the most important in industry: it is also the most difficult". Child (1969) has suggested that this was partly legitimatory in that by shifting the burden of responsibility on to the foreman managers saved themselves from some of the blame for any conflicts or misunderstandings that arose.

Although the pressure on the legitimacy of management was not maintained for long, management was no longer able to claim professional expertise as a justification for its existence. Instead the emphasis shifted to the manager as the leader of a team. At times the analogy was taken further, for example by Urwick (quoted in Child, 1969, p 129) who proposed as an aim the need to develop in workers the feeling "of belonging to an institution which is doing something worthwhile, the narrower sensation of belonging to a team. . . . We are all of us to some degree and in some respects children. We need someone to play the father to us".

This general picture serves to highlight the essentially

manipulative way in which human relations concepts were often put into practice. To protect their legitimacy management often preferred to offer the form rather than the substance. But there is no doubt that some managers saw the technical value of the team concept; others in the post-war era preferred to draw a parallel with the military. Such managers tried in various ways to put human relations into practice at a time when labour was scarce and effective utilization of the workforce was becoming essential.

The extensive practice of human relations led to a series of studies which were usually interpreted as supporting the social man perspective. Many of these focused on the role of the foreman and seemed to suggest that subordinates generally preferred him to be considerate, participative and subordinate-centred. However, the direct relationship between human relations and productivity was often disappointing. Likert (1961, 1967), who has for many years been one of the main advocates of human relations, accepts this criticism up to a point but emphasizes the long-term benefits. To illustrate these benefits, he has developed a system of human asset accounting which has many attractions for management. Although it may seem rather far removed from earlier human relations concepts, it is a direct development from them. There is no doubt that this approach, in the same way as scientific management, continues to be widely applied in industry in one form or another.

The social man perspective has provided three variations on direct participation of the worker in decision-making. The first is the result of participative leadership whereby subordinates are directly consulted about decisions affecting their day to day work. The second is the situation where the working group is given wide discretion to reach certain key decisions. The third stems from the communications system which provides the worker with the control to decide what sort of information he passes to his superiors, knowing that this information may influence the decisions which are taken.

A third distinctive management perspective which has emerged since the 1950s, has been described as the self-actualizing school (Schein) or the neo-human relations school (Child). It has a number of elements which distinguish it from the human relations school and which prevent it from being, as Child has implied, merely an extension of human relations. The first is its origin in the academic study of the needs of man. Whereas earlier perspectives were based on ideas and evidence derived mainly from industry, this movement owes its origins to psychiatrists and to a number of academic industrial consultants, several of whom had a bias towards clinical psychology.

The second element is that, with one notable exception (see Herzberg, 1966), it did not dismiss other ideologies as wrong: it preferred rather to see them as irrelevant to a modern industrial society. This is reflected in Maslow's hierarchy of needs (Maslow, 1943) which forms the theoretical basis for much of the movement.

A third factor, specific to this perspective, is an awareness of an ideology and of the possible influence of ideology. A curious contradiction remains because the whole approach minimizes the significance of extra-work influences on behaviour at work, yet is aware of the role of the industrial worker and of work itself in modern society. This awareness has led to certain strong criticisms of the essentially manipulative nature of the way in which human relations has been applied and, on a wider scale, of the role of industry in society. In this context, it is interesting that it is the larger, reputedly progressive organizations, often operating on an international scale, which have expressed most interest in intrinsic means of motivation.

A fourth distinguishing feature is that motivation and the desire to exert control are said to emanate from intrinsic sources within an individual and his relation to his job content rather than from extrinsic factors such as financial or social rewards and punishments. It is for this reason that we have termed this third perspective intrinsically motivated man.

In 1943 Maslow presented his views on motivation which discussed human needs in hierarchical terms. As we pointed out in Chapter 3, only an unsatisfied need was a motivator in his view; once this need had been satisfied, it was replaced by other less pressing needs. Maslow argued that these needs could be placed in an hierarchical order of prepotence, lower level needs being those which must be satisfied first. In ascending order these levels include:

1 Physiological needs
2 Safety and security needs
3 Social and affiliative needs
4 Ego satisfaction and status needs
5 Self-actualization needs.

Self-actualization is a state in which the individual makes full use of his capacity and potential for self-expression. It was seen originally by Maslow as a state to be reached only during a few peak periods in life. Furthermore Maslow was referring to needs in relation to the total life space of the individual and not necessarily or specifically to the work context.

These concepts were adapted and applied to industry by McGregor (1960). They form the basis for the management assumptions which he presents as Theory Y:

1 The expenditure of physical and mental effort in work is as natural as rest or play. The average human being does not dislike work. Depending upon controllable conditions, work may be a source of satisfaction or a source of punishment.
2 External controls and the threat of punishment are not the only means for bringing about effort towards organizational objectives. Man will exercise self-direction and self-control in the service of objectives towards which he is committed.
3 Commitment to objectives is a function of the rewards associated with their achievement. The most significant of

such rewards, eg the satisfaction of ego and self-actualizing needs, can be direct products of effort directed towards organizational objectives.

4 The average human being learns, under proper conditions, not only to accept but to seek responsibility.

5 The capacity to exercise a relatively high degree of imagination, ingenuity and creativity in the solution of organizational problems is widely, not narrowly, distributed in the population.

6 Under the conditions of modern industrial life, the intellectual potentialities of the average human being are only partially used.

Argyris (1964) reaches a similar position, stressing that the working man, in most spheres of his life, is primarily self-motivated and self-controlled. This is not so in industry and the external controls and sanctions cause a reaction towards immature and regressive behaviour. Since it is this pattern of behaviour that becomes the norm, management sees no evidence to cause it to change its ideas from Theory X which thereby, as we suggested earlier, becomes self-fulfilling. Maslow (1965) was rather more cautious in his acceptance of Theory Y. He was "a little worried about this stuff, which I consider to be tentative, being swallowed whole by all sorts of enthusiastic people" (1965, p 56). Although he was totally sympathetic towards McGregor's ideas and even suggested that they should be called Fact X and Fact Y, he was less certain about the generality of the application of Theory Y. He summed this up by saying "there is insufficient grounding for a firm and final trust in Theory Y management philosophy; but . . . there is even less firm evidence for Theory X" (1965, p 56).

This approach has a number of attractions for managers. As with the other major perspectives, it is essentially functionalist in its approach: the emphasis is on *Integrating the Individual and the Organization* (Argyris, 1964). By concentrating on the intrinsic aspects of the job, there is a tendency to ignore causes of conflict; in fact the implication is that conflict is regressive behaviour in a particular guise. The concern with the individual and the development of internal controls at the expense of a focus on the group level further implies that the role of unions is limited.

Another attraction for management, and one which is often stressed in the educational context, is that the notion of intrinsic motivation fits in with their own personal experience and their own motivational patterns. It is perhaps not surprising that much of the evidence for this approach is based on studies of managerial and professional levels.

Acceptance by management of this perspective calls for something of an act of faith. Although it may fit in with the manager's own behaviour, it is unlikely to conform to his experience of the way in which his workers behave. It implies that the manager must give up, to some extent at least, the traditional external controls and leave the workforce to display self-control and self-direction. A large body of evidence suggests that workers do not give high priority to the ability to exert greater control over their actual jobs. Against this it has been argued that contrary evidence of this type is based on studies of workers whose expectations have been conditioned by past events and who, in any case, have never been allowed to display extensive control over their work. In fact, so the argument sometimes goes, the worker does not really know what he wants; or as Neal and Robertson (1968) suggest, "he seeks, generally quite unconsciously, increased participation and an 'ownership' (as Drucker calls it) or control of his labour" (p 72). Discussing restrictive practices, they suggest that the worker "may still claim to be defending some battle that has long been decided in his favour, when in reality he is dimly endeavouring to give expression to a whole new series of wants, that he may be quite unaware of, but are nonetheless real for all that" (1968, p 73). Equally, it is argued that management must recognize that even an apparently militant workforce will accept managerial objectives once its basic needs have been satisfied and once it is given an opportunity to express intrinsic motivation. It is not surprising that many managers have felt that these pre-requisites are difficult to meet. This problem has been overcome, in theory at least, by Herzberg (1966), who claims that the causes of dissatisfaction and of satisfaction exist on different dimensions. This contradicts Maslow's notion of a hierarchy but suggests that intrinsic moti-vation can be tapped by operating on the 'satisfaction dimension' even in situations where dissatisfaction exists.

The key recommendation which emerges from the writ-ings of those who recommend the development of intrin-sic forms of motivation is that jobs and sometimes even whole organizations should be re-designed to fit the needs of the worker – and in particular to fit in with his needs for autonomy, responsibility and control. It is strongly argued that most of the existing jobs in industry and elsewhere do not provide the average worker with sufficient challenge or control. This problem will be overcome by 'enriching' the job and as a result the worker will perform more effectively and be more satisfied.

This perspective was initially accepted by managers who sought to raise productivity by fully motivating the workforce. In practice, management often ceded control over how a job was done; but they generally retained control, in outline at least, over the broader work objec-tives. More recently it has also come to assume a legiti-matory function as a means of demonstrating a sense of social responsibility to counter the arguments of those who are questioning the moral right of management to take away the meaning from work and to increase the control of the machine over the worker. It is also intended to support the combined technical and legiti-matory functions of channelling the desire for control into acceptable paths and away from a militant concern with the cash-nexus. In so far as it provides the worker with an element of control, this perspective leads to a form of direct participation.

COMPLEX MAN

Each of the three management perspectives we have described so far can be criticized for being too narrow and simplistic and for failing to explain the ever-increasing body of research evidence. To take account of these contradictions, Schein (1965) has suggested a fourth perspective – that of complex man. He provides five underlying assumptions:

1 Man's motives are highly complex and variable; they can change from time to time and from situation to situation according to circumstances.
2 Man can acquire new needs as a result of his experience. Therefore his behaviour within an organization is likely to be a function of his initial needs and his organizational experiences.
3 Man's motives can vary according to the organization or job with which he is involved.
4 Individual productivity and job satisfaction are dependent upon a number of factors. Motivation is only one of these; others include the nature of the work, the individual's ability and the required interaction with other workers.
5 Man can respond to many different managerial strategies and there is no single correct strategy for all workers at all times.

In some ways, this can be seen as a reaction against the prescriptive element in the other approaches. Instead it implies the need for careful analysis and diagnosis as a first step and for constant checking thereafter. Only then can a specific man-management strategy be recommended. Behavioural scientists and management consultants have been swift to offer advice on the kind of management style which is most appropriate to particular organizational contexts.

The variety of possibilities and the need for local diagnosis suits some managers who can act as judge and jury, justifying any style of management by claiming that it is the most appropriate to their particular case.

One approach which fits into this perspective and which is receiving growing attention is the use of an action frame of reference.[6] This argues that it is important to understand how the individuals in any situation define that situation and what factors influence their definition. Only by starting out from this viewpoint is it possible to explain social action. For example, because people have different backgrounds and, to some extent, different needs, they are likely to look at a particular situation from different viewpoints. In other words, the behaviour will be determined by the meanings they attach to the social structure.

The emergence of this approach can be traced back to a reaction against some of the more extreme forms of human relations. For example, Whyte's *Money and Motivation* (1955) highlighted the complexity of motivation in industry and pointed, in particular, to the importance of differences in social backgrounds and expectations. Subsequently academics who have provided process models of motivation (see, for example, Vroom, 1964) and management writers who have been particularly concerned with leadership (see for example, Fiedler, 1967) have helped to provide a wider discussion of this approach. However, it is likely to remain anathema to those managers who look for 'one best way'.

The complex man perspective does not have any specific implications for direct participation. However, by indicating the complexity of the problem, it can provide a framework within which to analyse the other approaches.

MANAGEMENT IN PRACTICE

In the previous sections, we have concentrated upon the development of managerial thinking in relation to worker participation; little is known about the extent to which the values of practising managers relate to those contained in the various perspectives. There are considerable difficulties in obtaining an accurate and detailed picture of how managers behave and relevant information is sparse. At least two notable studies (Hemphill, 1959; Stewart, 1967) have attempted to describe and classify managerial jobs on the basis of actual management behaviour. Neither provides the kind of detailed information on decision-making processes, particularly in relation to subordinates, which is required in the present context. Activity sampling of supervisors (see, for example, Wirdenius, 1958) comes closer to this. But no approach has successfully combined observation of what the manager does with an understanding of why he is doing it and how it relates to his management beliefs and values.

It is necessary to fall back on the available and less than satisfactory information on the relation between management ideology and management practice. One obvious source of information is the questionnaire which can be used to obtain either self-report data or subordinate and superordinate ratings of a manager's behaviour and values.[7] Self-report data in particular suffers from serious deficiencies in this context because it can often indicate what a manager likes to think he does or reflects what he feels his values ought to be in the eyes of other people and more especially in the eyes of his superiors and the investigator who is collecting the information. The existence of false or biased self-perception can be demonstrated through the use of the Blake Managerial Grid and associated training methods (Blake and Mouton, 1964).

Another major source of information is the statement of company ideology. Often this does no more than reflect pious hopes; the extent to which they are translated into practice may depend largely upon the enthusiasm of a few key senior managers. Hill (1971) has described some of the problems associated with the introduction of a new management philosophy in Shell UK Ltd. The statement of company philosophy was very much oriented towards the behavioural sciences and was drawn up with the help of the Tavistock Institute. Relevant sections emphasized the need to give each worker some element of challenge, control, decision-making and meaning in his job. In his evaluation of the success in implementing the philosophy, Hill emphasized the critical part played by top management in demonstrating its commitment and the role of influential change agents. He provides some evidence to suggest that the philosophy was successfully disseminated throughout the company but implies that it was subordinated to technical and operating requirements during any sort of crisis situation.

Cotgrove, Dunham and Vamplew (1971) have described the implementation of the Imperial Chemical Industries (ICI) company philosophy. They state that although it was essentially a wage-effort bargain "Company policy, however, attached considerable importance to the implications of the work of behavioural and social scientists, particularly the work of Herzberg and Likert indicating the importance of motivation and participation. Only a small nucleus of senior management was entirely convinced, but all agreed that the ideas were worth a try" (1971, p 45). It is clear that the level of commitment among managers in ICI has varied but that in certain sections of the organization there has been a determined effort to implement some of the changes implied in the agreement.

The overall significance of growth and profitability upon managerial attitudes is well illustrated in Nichols's (1969) study of a sample of northern businessmen. Definitions of the aim, role and perception of organizations were determined in relation to those objectives; for example, "conceptions of social responsibility did not necessitate the introduction of policies at odds with those general objectives of growth and profitability which it is to be expected that most companies will set themselves" (1969, p 225). In other words, the generally held view suggested that what was good for the company was also in the interest of the constituent groups who make up the organization. Social responsibility and, by implication, participation would be measured against criteria of profitability and growth. Shenfield (1971), in her study of company boards, found a similar emphasis upon profit. "None of the companies had any doubts that their primary objective was to be efficient and profitable and that being socially responsible would serve no useful purpose if it hindered these overall company goals" (1971, p 164).

THE SURVEY OF ATTITUDES TOWARDS PARTICIPATION

Because of the paucity of data about management views on participation, we have used the admittedly less satisfactory questionnaire approach with a sample of 90 middle level managers from a large nationalized concern in the non-manufacturing sector of industry. The great majority were aged between 35 and 50, were earning between £2,500 and £4,000 per annum in 1972 and had not been educated at university. As we were only hoping to obtain a general picture, and since the sample was small, we did not attempt any cross-tabulations on the basis of any of the biographical variables. We are not claiming that this group is in any way typical of the whole of British industry; indeed it must be borne in mind that the concern for which they worked has traditionally attracted a significant degree of commitment from its employees. Since our interest is in the direct forms of participation at shop floor level, the managers involved are practitioners rather than policy-makers. As such, they would constitute a key group in the implementation of participative techniques.

Each manager was given five sets of three statements. In each set he was asked to pick the one statement with which he most agreed. Most of the statements which were used were derived from comments made by similar groups of managers in earlier discussions on worker participation. The use of such statements has advantages in so far as they are realistic to the respondents, but they have drawbacks in that they can cover more than one issue in a single statement.

To obtain their perception of the role of management in

relation to the workforce, these managers were asked to select the statement with which they most closely agreed from those in Table 3. It can be seen that the majority rejected the more extreme viewpoints which consider the manager's role to be primarily one of maximizing profits or fulfilling social obligations. Like the managers in Nichols' (1969) sample, the majority felt that to optimize the company's long-term position, it was necessary to harmonize the economic needs of the organization with the social and economic needs of the worker. This viewpoint recognized the validity of objectives such as profitability and efficiency but implied that they could best be achieved by taking into account the rather different objectives of the workforce.

Table 3

A	The maximization of efficiency and profit should be a manager's sole concern, because it is the only true measure of managerial success.	16%
B	A manager should not simply concern himself with profit and efficiency because it would be to the advantage of the organization also to look after the social and economic needs of the worker	61%
C	A manager should not simply concern himself with profit and efficiency because he also has a moral duty to look after the social and economic needs of the worker	23%
		100%
	Number in sample	90

Consistent with this viewpoint, the majority agreed that there were competing interests between management and workforce. (It is interesting to compare this with the more strongly held teamwork image of Nichols' managers). Nevertheless, as Table 4 shows, it is quite clear that the

Table 4

A	To be successful, an organization must work like a football team with every-one pulling together. If everyone takes this view, there is no need for conflict of any sort between management and the workforce	25%
B	Industry represents a struggle between the conflicting interests of management and the workers. Therefore for any organization to be successful, manage-ment must be in a position of control over the workforce	7%
C	The interests of management and the workforce are often different. To be successful, an organization must main·tain a balance between these competing interests	68%
		100%
	Number in sample	88

managers in the sample do not want to be in a position of total domination and control.

The overall impression is that these managers see industry as being composed of differing interests and to be successful they must take them into account. The extent to which they take account of these differences will depend upon the circumstances. It can be seen from Table 5 that a sizeable minority believe that their expertise gives them the right to take decisions about the workforce. On the other hand, half of the managers would endeavour, at least in the first instance, to gain the prior approval of those affected.

Table 5

A	A manager reaches the position he is in by virtue of his expertise and ability. This expertise gives him the right to take decisions which affect the work-force	36%
B	Anyone who occupies a position of authority has a right to take decisions which affect the workforce	15%
C	No one, however competent and senior, has a right to take decisions which affect the workforce without first endeavouring to obtain its support	49%
		100%
	Number in sample	90

A somewhat similar division of views emerges on their attitudes towards the specific issue of worker participation. Thirty-five per cent adopt an instrumental approach whereby they consider that participation would only be acceptable if it led to greater efficiency. A further 28 per cent feel that some sort of participation is inevitable. Therefore, although there is a widespread acceptance of the existence of divergent interests, only a minority of managers feels that this, in itself, justifies the sharing of management decision-making among these interests. For the majority, worker participation is only justified if it is beneficial or inevitable.

Table 6

A	Workers should be allowed to have a say in managerial decisions only if it is likely to lead to greater efficiency	35%
B	Management should facilitate worker participation in managerial decisions, even if it has no impact on efficiency because workers have a right to control decisions which affect them	37%
C	Workers' participation in management must be allowed because the only way to manage is with the consent of the managed	28%
		100%
	Number in sample	89

MOTIVATION AND PARTICIPATION

A managerial philosophy which accepts the value of forms of direct participation such as job enrichment assumes that workers will respond positively if they are given additional responsibility and scope for achievement. This means that the individual will be motivated through the appropriate design of his job and not through an exclusive reliance on financial controls or forms of paternalism. Nevertheless, as

Table 7 shows, a majority of the managers rejected such a philosophy.

Although 32 per cent saw workers as only being interested in money, this proportion is more limited than that reported by Viteles (1953) in an American study. He found

Table 7

A	Basically, the only thing the majority of workers are interested in is money	32%
B	Most people will only work well if they like the people they work with and know that the company takes an interest in them	26%
C	Money is important up to a point, but what most workers really want is the chance to do a challenging and responsible job	42%
		100%
	Number in sample	90

that 44 per cent of executives felt that "money alone is the answer" in gaining worker productivity whilst a further 28 per cent felt that "it was by far the chief thing". A further 26 per cent of our managers emphasized social relations in the job; this corresponds closely with the number who believe that industrial relations can be viewed through the teamwork concept. Therefore only just over 40 per cent of our sample accept the theoretical concepts underlying the notions of intrinsic motivation which form the basis of much current management writing on direct participation.

Although it has not proved possible to indicate how far

the majority of managers accept one or other of the perspectives outlined in this chapter, we do know that in the last 10 years a rapidly increasing number has been introduced to current ideas about management. This is a result of the explosion in management training, stimulated primarily by the Industrial Training Act of 1964, which has helped to communicate the work of academics and consultants to practising managers. One consequence is that names such as Maslow, McGregor and Herzberg and the ideas associated with them are becoming increasingly widely known. These factors, coupled with the continuing debate on the social role of management, mean that more managers are confronted with the alternative ideologies; and since participation is usually a theme in such discussions, we cannot afford to ignore the subject.

Summary

In this chapter we have suggested that managers will have certain beliefs about how to manage and these will be reflected in their views on worker participation. Although in the great majority of managers such beliefs rest at the sub-conscious level, a number have put their ideas into writing. In looking at such writing, a distinction can be made between its technical and legitimatory functions. The technical aspects deal with how managers should manage and the legitimatory aspects deal with why managers should manage.

It is possible to distinguish three main management perspectives, all of which permit some form of direct participation. The economic man perspective, derived largely from the ideas of engineers like Taylor (1947) provided a technique which came to be known as scientific management; this was based on the careful measurement of work followed by the use of incentive payment schemes. It was viewed as legitimatory by those managers who sought to base their position on expertise and by some who hoped that 'scientific' measurement would obviate the need for union bargaining. It provided a major opportunity for direct participation by allowing workers to control the extent to which they responded to the incentive.

The social man perspective is often thought to stem from the Hawthorne Studies (Roethlisberger and Dickson, 1939) but its roots can be traced back to the period just after the first world war. It is based on the assumption that workers develop an informal social group which has a major influence on performance. Management should ensure that the group is cooperative by insisting upon open communications, participative leadership and group involvement in decision-making. This provides the technical framework and in so far as it is presented as management by consent, it also provides legitimacy. It leads to direct participation because in practice it implies some ceding of control to the workers.

The third perspective, intrinsically motivated man, has been strongly influenced by Maslow's (1943) concept of a hierarchy of needs and is based on the assumption that the majority of workers in industry today will respond primarily to intrinsic or job content factors. The technical implication of this is that jobs should be re-designed or enriched to make them more interesting and to give the worker greater control. It therefore provides a strategy for dealing with technological change and has implications for legitimacy in so far as management can claim that it is providing workers with what they really want out of a job. Since the re-design of jobs should provide the worker with more control, this again constitutes a form of direct participation.

A number of managers may prefer a fourth perspective known as complex man. This suggests that people have varying needs and motives and therefore the critical requirement is to develop an effective strategy for diagnosing a particular situation.

There is little clear evidence on management behaviour and attitudes in relation to participation, although a number of organizations have developed an ideology and made

93

some attempt to put it into practice. To gain some further insight into the attitudes of practising managers, we asked 90 to complete a questionnaire. While they rejected the view of the manager as a profit maximizer, profitability and variability were considered to be the primary goals of the organization. Participation seemed to be viewed as an aid to management rather than as a desirable objective in its own right.

NOTES

1 A major exception has been the Institute of Workers Control which advocates direct participation and total worker control of all aspects of the ownership and management of organizations.

2 A notable exception has been the work of Brown (1962) and Jaques (1961). In their analysis of the Glacier Company they realized that the incentive scheme represented a loss of management control and developed in its place a job evaluation scheme known as the time-span of discretion. Although it was a product of the 1950s it has close affinities to Taylor's scientific management. Basically, it argued that men are able, intuitively, to judge their worth; this perceived fair pay can be measured on the time span of discretion. The time span of discretion was a neutral tool, like scientific management and also, like scientific management, remained in the control of managers rather than workers.

3 In so far as contentious incentive payment schemes provide a fertile ground for bargaining, this strategy is also likely to lead to unexpected increases in indirect, as well as direct, participation.

4 Baldamus (1961) in his discussion of the effort-bargain, defines positive disparity as disparity in favour of the workers rather than management. Roy takes a cue from the workers in his study and talks of 'gravy jobs'.

5 Roy (1952) has argued that where the worker fears that management may adjust the piece-rate, he will seek to retain a positive disparity by keeping output below a rate where management would be likely to perceive the rate as being too generous.

6 For a fuller discussion of the implications of the Action Frame of Reference, see Silverman, D (1970). It is also dealt with more fully in subsequent chapters.

7 Many of the relevant findings on management style are described in chapter 6 on Social Controls.

CHAPTER FIVE

CONTROL THROUGH INCENTIVE PAYMENT SCHEMES

Our analysis of control has indicated that restrictive practices could constitute a significant form of direct participation. This chapter examines the scope for the exercise of control by workers through restriction of output. The focus is directed primarily towards restriction of output in relation to incentive payment schemes, but other forms of restrictive practice often associated with a concern for job security and the maintenance of effective social relations are also considered. Five major reasons for restricting output are identified and the evidence relating to them is assessed.

THE USE OF FINANCIAL INCENTIVES IN INDUSTRY

Those who accept the philosophy of scientific management and the concept of economic man assume that money is the major inducement both to come to work and, once there, to work hard and that financial incentives are the most effective means of motivating the workforce. The general lack of evidence about management attitudes makes it difficult to know how widely accepted these views are although of the managers referred to in chapter 4, only 32 per cent considered workers to be solely motivated by money. Some information can be obtained by examining the payment methods in industry but Shimmin (Marriott, 1968), reviewing this subject, admitted that it is difficult to determine the extent to which various systems are used. Estimates of the proportion of organizations using incentive schemes varied from 33 per cent (Ministry of Labour, 1961) to 83 per cent (Institution of Works Managers, 1966) and 84 per cent

(Corner, 1967). These last two studies covered a relatively small and somewhat unrepresentative sample and not all of the organizations making up the figure used incentives with all of the workforce. It is also possible that the term 'incentive payment scheme' may have been variously interpreted or that different terms were used. In the present context we are concerned with situations in which a significant proportion of a worker's wage is based upon his performance. Often these are referred to as schemes of payment by results. Evidence indicates that 'significant' can generally be taken to mean at least one quarter of total earnings.

Research Paper No 10 to the Royal Commission on Trade Unions and Employers Associations (McCarthy and Parker, 1968) provided some further evidence. It reported a survey of workers, shop stewards, foremen and managers. Thirty per cent of the random sample of union members said they operated with a system of payment by results.[1] Among the shop stewards, who were drawn from six unions, 26 per cent said that all, and 14 per cent that most, of their members came under payment by results schemes; 55 per cent said that none of their members was paid by this method. The extent to which payment by result schemes were used, and presumably the type of system used, varied considerably from one industry to another; 59 per cent of shop stewards in the distributive trades said all or most of their members were paid in this way compared with only seven per cent of those responsible for members in professional and scientific jobs (Government Social Survey, 1968). In the section of the survey covering the responses of managers, 79 per cent of the plants covered had a system of payment by results; in 90 per cent of the cases, these covered all or most of the workforce; 63 per cent of the foremen included in the survey reported that all or most of those they supervised were paid by results. Despite the wide differences between the responses of the various samples, it is still possible to conclude that the use of incentive payments is still widespread.

97

American evidence is also extremely scarce. Lawler (1971) reports a 1940 survey by the National Industrial Conference Board as his main, and most recent, source of information. This showed that 51·7 per cent of the sample of 2,700 organizations used wage-incentive schemes. The widespread use elsewhere of systems of payment by results is indicated in a more recent report on the subject from Sweden, normally regarded as one of the countries with the most progressive policies, which opens with the statement "Payment by results is the most common remuneration form for workers" (SAF, 1972, p 5).

FINANCIAL INCENTIVES AND CONTROL

The assumptions underlying the relationship between incentive schemes and worker control can be analysed in the context of the expectancy model presented in chapter 3. This would suggest that if the financial rewards sufficiently outweigh the costs of trying to attain them, and the individual feels that by his own efforts he can achieve these rewards, his motivation and his effort-input will be high.

The worker has control to the extent that he can often vary his effort-input. This only has an impact when such action determines either the pace or the quality of his work, but preferably both. Management allows the worker this freedom on the assumption that his most pressing needs are satisfied by money and that no competing needs are strong enough to stand in the way. Since the validity of this whole approach depends, in the first instance, upon the correctness of this management assumption, we turn next to a discussion of the importance of money and of other job factors.

THE IMPORTANCE OF PAY

One way of examining the importance of pay is to ask people either to say how important it is in itself or how important it is in comparison with other factors. This approach and the way in which it has often been used present a number of dangers. First, it does not tell us why money is important; secondly, we must know in what context it is important since there is evidence to suggest that it may be important when considering whether or not to apply for a job, but less so once one is in the job; thirdly, when pay is being compared with other factors, its importance will depend partly upon what it is being compared with. Finally the data is based upon a snapshot. Social situations change and are constantly redefined by those involved, thereby potentially limiting the validity of the information over a period of time. The following discussion can therefore be taken as no more than a broad indicator of the significance of pay. Lawler (1971) has reported 49 studies dealing with the importance of pay: almost all of them were conducted in the United States and the approaches are so diverse that comparison is rendered almost meaningless. On average, pay emerged as the third most important factor. This gives it considerably more prominence than it has sometimes been assumed to have. Some studies (see for example, Herzberg *et al,* 1957; Jurgensen,[2] 1948) have placed it lower down the list but Opsahl and Dunnette (1966), in their critical review of such studies, have offered a number of reasons why pay should receive such an apparently lowly rating. They cite three main reasons: first, they suggest that the reinforcement provided by saying money is important on a questionnaire is different and presumably less than the actual reinforcement which it provides in real life. However, they ignore the fact that this may hold equally true for other factors. Secondly, they suggest that many people are incapable of judging accurately what they really do want. Once again, this can operate to make pay – and any other factor – more or less important. Thirdly, they argue that there may be a social desirability response which encourages people to say that money is less important than it really is. Bendig and Stillman (1958) cite a further possible influence: the environmental factors which operate at the time the rating is made; in particular, a person who is dissatisfied with his pay and is constantly aware of this dissatisfaction will probably attach more importance to it than someone who is perfectly satisfied with his earnings and has little cause to give them constant consideration.

In the British studies cited by Opsahl and Dunnette (Wilkins 1949, 1950; Graham and Sluckin 1954), pay is ranked second and first in importance respectively. These findings suggest that if a social desirability response is operating in the United Kingdom, it does not necessarily operate in the same direction as it does in the USA. Our own studies would tend to bear this out. These have made use of the same questionnaire on a number of different populations and have been based mainly on the factors isolated by Herzberg (1966).

Table 8 lends broad support to the concept of a hierarchy of needs (Maslow, 1943) which corresponds to occupational level. Blue-collar workers attach priority to deficiency needs such as pay, job security and inter-personal relations. Supervisors show fairly similar priorities but attach more importance to growth factors such as the opportunity for achievement. Finally, managers are primarily concerned with growth factors. It is possible to conclude from this data that pay is a critical factor for both railmen and dockers and for their supervisors. But job security and interpersonal relations are almost as important as pay and must be taken fully into account when considering reasons for attempting to exert control.

Items such as pay, security and interpersonal relations differ from aspects of job content in one important respect. Job content factors such as achievement, responsibility and recognition are generally complementary and each supports the other. But extrinsic factors may quite clearly conflict with each other. In particular, attempts to optimize pay can lead to conflict with the needs for job security and acceptable interpersonal relations. This further emphasizes the fact that these items cannot be examined in isolation.

THE NATURE OF THE EFFORT-BARGAIN

Without necessarily making conscious decisions, the worker will try to optimize the various important outcomes

Table 8

Importance of Pay in Relation to other Factors (Rank Order)

	Unskilled railway workers	Dockers	Railway supervisors	Dock supervisors	Dock managers	Military officers	Railway[3] managers
	n* = 52	40	30	43	23	125	24
Interpersonal relations	1	3	1	2=	8=	7	7=
Pay	2	1=	2	2=	6=	3	4=
Job security	3	1=	4	1	5	5	6
The work itself	4	7=	5	6	1	1	3
Opportunity for achievement	5	5	3	2=	4	2	1
Responsibility	6=	10	6	7	2	4	2
Supervision	6=	4	7	11	12	10	12
Company policy and administration	9	6	13	8	8=	12	11
Working conditions	8	7=	9	5	13	13	10
Recognition	11	9	12	10	6=	9	7=
Promotion	10	13	8	9	3	6	4=
Personal life	12	11	11	12	10	8	13
Status	13	12	10	13	11	11	9

* *n* = the number in each sample.

available to him; if possible, he will control and vary his effort-input to achieve this. Behrend (1957) and Baldamus (1961) have used the concept of the effort-bargain to analyse attempts to exert control in this way. The effort-bargain is concerned with the relationship between the effort-input and the various rewards. When this relationship is perceived to be fair there is a state of parity, but at other times this can vary on the side of either positive or negative disparity. When the disparity increases beyond an acceptable level, attempts are likely to be made to return to a state of parity. The worker can attempt to do this by controlling his effort, either through restriction of output or, in more extreme cases, by withdrawing his labour altogether. The location of the parity line will be determined by individual perceptions; these perceptions will, in turn, be influenced by a wide range of pressures, including the attitudes of co-workers, so that it may sometimes become more relevant to talk in terms of group perception. Since the factors influencing the perception of a fair effort-bargain can vary almost from day to day, and are likely to alter fundamentally over a longer period of time, it is more useful to think in terms of a dynamic parity line.

This type of analysis highlights the potential conflict which exists in any industrial situation. Equally it implies that the worker recognizes this conflict and expects a manipulative management strategy since "as wages are costs to the firm, and the deprivations inherent in the effort mean 'costs' to the employee, the interest of management and wage-earners are diametrically opposed in terms of the disparity process . . ." (Baldamus, 1961, p 105). This expectation of conflict can mean that even where there is a perceived positive disparity in favour of the worker (or management) he will if possible use his control to exploit the situation and prevent management from re-establishing a state of parity. In other words, he will store up his 'weapons' in the conflict. This process has been highlighted in the studies of Roy (1952, 1953 and 1955) and Lupton (1963). There are various parallels between this effort-bargain approach and equity theory. Jaques (1961), for example, has argued that workers have a concept of fair pay based on what he calls 'the time span of discretion'. This, as its name implies, is a measure of the amount of responsibility exercised by an individual. He further suggests that workers strive for equity rather than a state of 'positive disequilibrium' since the latter can produce feelings of guilt. The theory cannot therefore accommodate purely instrumental and opportunistic bargaining of the type we have just outlined.

WHY WORKERS SEEK CONTROL THROUGH RESTRICTIONS OF OUTPUT

Although the payment system provides the opportunity for control, pay may not always be the reason for seeking control. We have suggested that pay, job security and interpersonal relations are often key factors and this seems particularly likely when incentive payment schemes are in operation. Summarizing a number of studies, Viteles (1953) has provided a more detailed list of reasons why a worker might want to control output. His list includes fear of rate cuts, resentment against a speed-up of work, attempts to postpone redundancies, attempts to stabilize earnings, attempts to secure steady employment, a means of airing grievances, general anti-management feelings, general discouragement, the belief that profits are too high, protection of less competent workers and a lack of confidence in standards. Whyte (1955) has added some further reasons including the response to group pressures and the general desire to exert control, both as an end in itself and as a means of influencing management.

Whether or not the worker actually needs to protect himself, it seems that he invariably reacts as if he feels that he does. Marriott (1968) explains the reasoning: "If it is true that as soon as workers became the paid servants of others, restriction of output appeared, and that its roots lie deep in human nature, it is not surprising that it is around this one factor that much industrial strife has taken place. The implication is that where freedom is curtailed the individual feels impelled to resist in some way" (1968, p 181).

In reviewing the studies on restriction of output, it seems that the reasons cited by Viteles and others can be reduced in number and broadened into more general categories.

1 Restriction to protect an existing rate or to promote a new one.
2 Restriction in response to group pressures: although the group leaders may have certain objectives in setting group norms, it is not so much to attain them as in response to group pressures that restriction takes place.
3 Restriction as a means of control over the individual's immediate work environment.
4 Restriction to protect job security.
5 Restriction as a means of influencing management in the general bargaining situation.

RESTRICTION TO PROTECT AN EXISTING RATE OR PROMOTE A NEW ONE

There is fairly wide agreement that it is almost impossible to set an entirely objective piece-rate (see Shimmin, 1968). In theory, every piece-rate can be regarded as either tight or loose, fair or unfair, depending upon the viewpoint of the observer. If workers feel that it is tight, they will endeavour to persuade management to adjust it to a more equitable level. Roy (1952) has shown how workers try to achieve this through 'quota restriction', whereby they lower their output and their earnings in the short-term hoping to persuade management to ease the rate and provide them with long-term gains. At the other extreme there are what Roy called 'gravy' jobs which had a loose rate and a potential for high earnings. But since it was accepted that management would tighten a rate which appeared to be loose, a policy of 'goldbricking' was practised. This was a process whereby output and earnings were increased only to the point where it was felt that management would not notice that the rate was loose. Anyone who increased output beyond this point was subjected to strong group pressures to return to acceptable levels.

In a different context, Lupton (1963), again through participant observation, described how men producing electrical transformers operated 'the fiddle' on certain jobs to control the speed of the work so that earnings could be optimized. When the rate was acceptable, they would work hard at the job; when it was not, they devised various means of claiming extra time and allowances.

The need to protect or fight for a fair rate highlights the inequalities that often seem to be an inevitable feature of payment by results. Despite the possible attractions of the control provided by such schemes, workers are therefore forced from time to time to weigh up the rewards and costs inherent in them and a number have concluded that greater advantages are to be derived from a more stable system. In Sweden there is evidence of pressure in this direction from the workers (SAF, 1972). In the United Kingdom, moves by management have attracted more attention. The Government Social Survey (1968) found that over half the shop stewards with members on payment by results would prefer a different payment system, mainly to avoid the fluctuations and inequalities of payment by results. It is perhaps surprising that only 30 per cent of the sample of workers in the survey expressed similar attitudes. Management and foremen were even more ready to see the advantages of payment by results and there was a slightly larger proportion in favour of introducing rather than abandoning such schemes.

RESTRICTION IN RESPONSE TO GROUP PRESSURES

Although workers as a group may have a specific reason for controlling production levels, they can sometimes reach the stage where group norms and group standards become ends in themselves. A work group can exist for both technical and social reasons but its continued existence as a social entity may become an end in itself. This notion of a set of shared values which are based on the social standards of the group, and which may differ from management's values and expectations in relation to output, was used by the Hawthorne researchers to explain restriction of output. Mayo (1933) implied that this led to an unconscious, almost irrational restriction of output rather than a deliberate attempt to control the environment in competition with management. This approach has been strongly criticized by a number of writers (see, for example, Lupton, 1963) for its naivety. Although these criticisms are valid, they do not destroy the argument that the workers may choose to restrict output for purposes relating to the functions of the social group rather than for reasons connected with attempts to control their rewards or control their job content.

Dalton (Whyte, 1955) conducted a detailed study of a group of workers to discover the reasons for restriction of output and the influences on their behaviour. He isolated three groups: those who restricted output more extensively than the group norm and whom he termed restrictors; those who stuck fairly closely to the norm; and rate-busters who exceeded the norm. He discovered that the group to which an individual belonged was determined largely by factors in his social background. Those who attached particular value to the group and to status within the group were often to be found among the extreme restrictors. They tended to have an urban background, to come from a fairly close-knit community in which group values were dominant and to have a fairly low level of aspiration. In contrast, the rate-busters tended to have a more rural, individualistic upbringing and did not share the values of the urban group and its background community. Their values were closer to those of management and in particular they had a high level of aspiration.

Roethlisberger and Dickson's (1939) account of the Hawthorne studies again highlighted the power and influence of the work group as an entity in itself. Status levels within the informal group were found to be quite different from those of the formal authority structure. Status within the informal system was reflected in certain codes of behaviour such as general non-cooperation with management and tight control over the accepted level of output. Both were strongly reinforced by group sanctions. The critics of the Hawthorne studies (see, for example, Landsberger, 1958) have pointed out that restriction of output in the bank wiring room[4] can be attributed in part to the depression in the American economy and fear of redundancies. However, the evidence suggested that quite apart from this, control over output was exerted as part of the social *raison d'etre* of the group.

Both these studies suggest that social values develop which encourage restriction of output, quite apart from the many other reasons for it that may exist.

RESTRICTION AS A MEANS OF CONTROL OVER THE IMMEDIATE WORK ENVIRONMENT

Incentive payment schemes which leave the worker with some freedom over the pacing of his work offer some unintended opportunities to exert control over items in his immediate work environment. These can include freedom from close supervision, freedom from machine pacing and freedom to choose whether or not to accept the challenge offered by management and respond to the incentive scheme. Roy (1952) has shown how some individuals worked hard for periods in an attempt to store up free time which they could use largely as they pleased. This time was occasionally used to flaunt their idleness in front of supervisors, both to show up the lack of authority of the supervisors and to demonstrate their nonchalant attitude towards management's financial incentives. A similar reaction has been noted in tightly controlled work contexts such as the car production line (Walker and Guest, 1952) where the policy of 'banking' was practised. There are likely to be large individual differences in attitudes towards control of this type; some of these differences are explored in chapter 9.

RESTRICTION OF OUTPUT TO PROTECT JOB SECURITY

A threat to job security also threatens both payment levels and interpersonal relations at work: one would therefore predict that the worker will exert whatever control he can to eliminate such a threat. It is now fairly widely accepted that the basically exploitative nature of certain incentive payment schemes encourages a concern for job security. Taylor himself blamed many of the failures of early schemes on management's over-willingness to adjust rates or eliminate surplus manpower when production increased. Landsberger (1958) attributed the restriction of output in the bank wiring room at the Hawthorne plant partly to a fear for job security.

Certain types of incentive scheme encourage restriction of output because financial security is threatened by unstable earnings. The evidence of Hickson (1963), Buiter (1964) and others suggests that workers prefer stable earnings to a fluctuating income, even though the logical implication is to move on to a fixed weekly wage. An unstable and unpredictable work-flow lends itself to restriction of output. This was identified as one of the major problems existing in British docks when men were employed on a casual basis. Men were employed for half-day periods and, even if there was only a few minutes work to be done, this still meant half a day's earnings. The obvious consequence was that when there was unlikely to be any highly paid work available in the next period, the previous job was stretched out to ensure that it lasted into the vacant period. The same sort of system applied with overtime, which in some cases lasted a minimum of two hours: the job could be stretched out until overtime working was agreed and then quickly finished off once the two hours of overtime earnings were guaranteed.

On a wider scale serious threats to job security can be countered in a variety of ways: coal miners and dockers in the United Kingdom provide contrasting examples. Both have had a long tradition of militancy, but militancy at the local rather than the national level. Over the years, miners reacted to the threatened closure of pits in two main ways.

One was to substitute group action, such as strikes, for individual action in the form of higher absenteeism and labour turnover. Turner (1969) has suggested that absenteeism was particularly costly to the industry because of its extent and its unpredictable nature. The other reaction was to attempt to raise production to an economic level to justify keeping open pits threatened with closure. There was no restriction of output and only limited conflict with management at the local level; in places such as South Wales, the threat was just as real to the local management whose home was in the same valley community as the miners. The most significant result of this was that the closure of many mines was carried through with comparatively little difficulty. In the docks, the main aim was to cut down the number of jobs rather than close down sections of the industry. Faced with over-manning and a contracting amount of labour intensive work, the dockers put the blame on the traditional inefficiency of management and refused to cooperate. Their position was strengthened by the type of management weakness which, for example, had allowed the 'welt' to exist in the Liverpool docks, whereby only half a gang worked at any one time. The dockers restricted output and refused to work new mechanized systems until they had successfully guaranteed either their job security or an acceptable financial pay-off.

If job security, in its broadest sense, is seen to be threatened in any way, the workforce will use its potential control to influence the situation. The way in which this control is used will depend upon the strategy which appears to have the greatest chance of success. This may take the form of restriction of output or it may also manifest itself in the other restrictive practices which are outlined later in this chapter.

RESTRICTION OF OUTPUT AS A MEANS OF INFLUENCING THE BARGAINING SITUATION

Various forms of restrictive practice can be used as a means of influencing the bargaining situation. Practices such as restriction of entry in industries are probably more prevalent than restriction of output in this context. Few studies have inquired specifically into the impact of restriction of output on negotiating behaviour. However, analysis of certain productivity bargains has indicated an awareness of the advantages of possessing practices which can be 'bought off'. For example, some evidence from the Esso refinery at Fawley has suggested that although the initial productivity bargain cut out a lot of overtime, in subsequent years the amount of overtime working gradually crept up again. And workers in sections of British Leyland extracted a high price from management for the abandonment of their piece-rate system.

The potential role of restriction of output in the bargaining situation has been highlighted in Walton and McKersie's (1965) analysis of bargaining situations. In any conflict there is a tendency towards what they call distributive bargaining or bargaining which is primarily concerned with 'dividing the cake'. To succeed in this, it is often necessary to destroy the opponent's case and, if possible, to alter his perception both of the underlying situation and of his chances of success. In this context, restriction of output may be used as an overt bargaining ploy or it may be a covert way of misleading management into believing that they are setting unfair rates.

OTHER TYPES OF RESTRICTIVE PRACTICE

In discussing restriction of output, we have inevitably had to introduce other restrictive practices and we turn now to examine these in a little more detail. Research Paper No 4 of the Royal Commission on Trade Unions and Employers Associations (1967) included a section on this subject. It defined a restrictive labour practice as "an arrangement under which labour is not used efficiently and which is not justifiable on social grounds" (1967, p 47). This left the subject open to dispute since what to the worker may seem a socially justifiable protective practice may be seen as blatant and unjustified restriction by management. There are circumstances in which management condones restrictive practices; for example, it is not uncommon for management to allow overtime in the belief that this encourages workers to remain with the organization. Research Paper No 4 (1967) also highlighted restrictive practices which were not actively sought by workers but which were allowed by inefficient management; examples included bad time-keeping and excessive tea breaks. Management may also permit a limited amount of absenteeism which, in certain circumstances, can represent a rather more extreme form of individual action to restrict output.

The purpose of the major restrictive practices is invariably related to at least one of the three key factors of pay, interpersonal relations and job security with particular emphasis on job security.[5] Some illustrations will help to demonstrate this. Demarcation lines set limits on the scope of the work which particular types of worker can do and generally lead to inefficient use of manpower. This is often seen as a move by craftsmen to protect their status and security in a time of technological change, but it can apply equally well to solicitors and barristers or to stevedores and dockers. Craftsmen's mates still exist in sections of industry and can lead to serious under-utilization of manpower if they are not given a job of their own. This again is primarily a means of protecting job security in much the same way as the restriction of entry which exists in some industries. Overmanning, which has been particularly prevalent in the printing industry, can be seen as a means of using the power of the work group and the trade union to protect security.

Restrictive practices can develop into more overt forms of control in times of open industrial conflict. Management can act by banning overtime in a situation in which it is accepted practice to work overtime. Workers may refuse to handle certain goods or materials, either to aid their own bargaining or as a way of expressing sympathy with other workers. In some industries a work to rule can cause serious disruptions and delays. All these are relatively short-term forms of behaviour which generally have a specific objective in the context of a bargaining situation. However, they demonstrate the way in which restrictive practices may be the first step on the path to other forms of action.

One other form of direct action which has been tried at various times during this century, and which has returned to favour in the early 1970s is the sit-in or work-in. Bishop (1973) reports that there were more than 70 in the United Kingdom during 1971 and 1972. Usually they represent a protest against the proposed closure of a factory or workplace and are therefore a means of defending job security. Despite the dramatic success of the workers at Upper Clyde Shipbuilders, subsequent efforts have produced mixed results. But where all else has failed, and their livelihood is threatened, some workers are likely to feel that this approach is justified; in this context it certainly has a greater chance of success than a strike which might simply speed the closure. Sit-ins have also been used, mainly by the Engineering Union, as a tactic in wage bargaining but here they seem to have had limited success.

THE SIGNIFICANCE OF RESTRICTIVE PRACTICES AS A MEANS OF WORKER CONTROL

This chapter has discussed the nature and purpose of restriction of output and, to a lesser extent, other types of restrictive practice. In industry as a whole, restrictive practices probably provide the most easily available means whereby workers can exert control. Two further points must therefore be developed. The first relates to the extent to which restrictive practices exist throughout industry; it is clearly impossible to gain accurate information about this and often the seriousness of restrictive practices must be inferred from management concern about them. The second point deals with how far what appear to be restrictive practices are, in fact, conscious attempts to exert some form of control.

Research Paper No 4 (1967) concluded by confirming that it was virtually impossible to provide an accurate assessment of the extent of restrictive practices. One major difficulty was the definition, which makes the only reasonable assessment that of an outsider using specified criteria. The Paper agrees with Clegg (1964), who felt that the problem was an extremely serious one. The improvements produced by productivity deals, even in what were often thought to be relatively efficient organizations, are cited as under-utilization of human resources although it is questionable whether this is always the result of workers' attempts to restrict output. Reviewing the evidence, Whyte (1955) concluded that probably less than 10 per cent of the workforce are giving their full effort towards the achievement of organizational goals. On the other hand, Roberts (1967) has argued that in shipbuilding and ship repairing the impact of various demarcation practices on productivity is minimal.

In the Government Social Survey, 40 per cent of works managers and 51 per cent of personnel officers claimed that there were restrictive practices in their plant. The main examples were extended breaks, slow working, bad time-keeping and demarcation issues. Almost three-quarters of managers and 43 per cent of foremen, but only 30 per cent of workers, thought that workers could reasonably be expected to exert more effort towards higher productivity. The main reasons for the apparent lack of effort were seen as being a lack of financial incentive, laziness and lack of interest. In other words, they saw the issue in terms of apathy rather than deliberate policy on the part of workers.

The general consensus seems to be that restrictive

practices can present a serious problem for management, although the Social Survey sample indicated that their elimination would result in savings of labour costs per unit of output of well under 20 per cent. The degree to which this 'problem' is caused by the deliberate efforts of the workforce cannot be accurately assessed. Despite the comments of managers cited above, the majority of research reports which have investigated the subject in any detail provide evidence of some deliberate attempts to exert control by at least part of the workforce. This may be why the study was reported or why the investigation was conducted in the first place; it is difficult to know whether the organizations concerned are the exceptions or, as is perhaps more likely, merely the tip of the iceberg.

Zweig (1951) has suggested that it is necessary to take into account and assess the extent of 'the restrictive spirit . . .' Similarly, Lupton (1963) has tried to analyse what he calls the workers will to control and to establish the circumstances under which such a will is most likely to manifest itself. Although this could be a useful approach, he related it too closely to his own case studies and tended to draw general conclusions from them. He distinguished between factors internal and external to the organization and included such matters as the nature of the market, the power of the unions, identification with management and the method of payment.

Since restriction of output hinges largely upon the payment system, a number of writers (Marriott, 1968 and Opsahl and Dunnette, 1966) have tried to analyse the conditions under which an incentive payment scheme will be successful. Marriott, (1968) listed 31 factors which various writers have specified as essential for the success of a scheme. Four of them seem likely to be particularly important:

1 there must be a clearly perceived relation between effort and reward
2 the system must be fair and must be seen to be fair

3 the system must be clearly understood by all those involved
4 the amount of the incentive must be seen as worthwhile.

But even these are not always relevant variables and the
evidence remains rather ambiguous. Nevertheless, the
majority of schemes are unlikely to meet all these criteria, in
which case either the 'will to control' or apathy is likely
to be present. Pym (1964) has emphasized the problem
by noting that incentive payment schemes have been in
operation almost everywhere where social scientists have
observed restrictive practices.

The attitudes and fears underlying the 'will to control' are
highlighted in two surveys conducted by the Opinion
Research Corporation in the United States. In the first
(ORC, 1949), 50 per cent of those covered felt that an
increase in output would be bad for them. In the second
(Viteles, 1953), 30 per cent of the workers felt that higher
productivity would lead to higher quotas, 11 per cent felt it
would lead to lower piece-rates, 23 per cent felt it would be
unpopular with other workers and only a small percentage
felt it would lead to no change of any sort.

That what appears to be a restrictive practice is really no
more than a sign of apathy or laziness is the alternative
possibility. In theory this would be most likely to occur
where there is a weak relationship between effort, performance and reward. A different perspective is offered by
Baldamus (1961) in his analysis of effort. He isolated three
major distastes involved in repetitive work and termed
them impairment, tedium and weariness. On the other hand
he argued that boring, repetitive work can also produce
some relative satisfactions, which contrast with the three
distastes and which he termed inurement, traction and
contentment. Inurement is the state of adaptation to unpleasant working conditions; traction is the "feeling of
being pulled along by the inertia inherent in a particular
activity" (1961, p 59); and contentment is a feeling of being
in the mood for work. Traction is the most important of

these; it implies that certain jobs have a natural rhythm and that to slow or to break this rhythm leads to a feeling of relative stress. Although this must be weighed against the satisfaction of controlling the work pace, the approach raises the question of whether restrictive practices introduce deprivations other than the more obvious ones, such as a short-term sacrifice of income. It also leads to the possibility that the easiest path may sometimes be to accept a swift, steady work rhythm.

Evidence on the potential stress involved in restricting output, represented for example by the findings of Dalton's study[6] (Whyte, 1955), coupled with the more overt financial sacrifices which may be required, and the evidence from most studies that the workers were fully aware of what they were doing, lends credence to the argument that restriction involves certain 'costs'. Group pressures and the influence of group leaders are likely to be potent factors in encouraging restrictive behaviour and Dalton's study suggests that the costs of contravening group norms can sometimes appear to be greater than the costs of restricting output. Because perceptible costs are involved and clear-cut alternatives are often available, it is likely that restriction of output associated with incentive payment schemes is usually the result of deliberate action by the workers.

Summary

This chapter has examined the scope for control offered to the workforce by a management decision to use incentive payment schemes. These schemes are based on the assumption that money is the most important incentive available and that by giving workers sufficient control to enable them to earn more money, they will exert more effort and thereby satisfy both their own needs for higher earnings and management's need for higher productivity. However, the available evidence from the United Kingdom indicates that job security and satisfactory interpersonal relations are often equally important factors. Therefore where either pay, job security or interpersonal relations are threatened, restrictive practices are likely to operate. Although restriction of output represents the most obvious day to day means of controlling performance, other restrictive practices, such as rigid demarcation, excessive overtime, lengthy tea-breaks and overmanning, are widely found.

There seem to be at least five main reasons for restriction of output: to protect or alter existing rates of pay; to respond to group pressures; to control the working environment; to protect job security; and to influence a more general bargaining situation. Restriction of output is a significant form of control both because it is widespread and because, in the short-term at least, it means a financial sacrifice. The workers can hardly fail to be aware of this and therefore are likely to make a conscious decision to exert this control. This helps to refute the argument that what appears to be restriction of output is often no more than apathy or laziness. At the same time, we must not forget that, in certain circumstances, the workforce will use this control as expected by management to optimize earnings and output.

Given that restriction of output is widespread and deliberate, it is ironic that a strategy used by management to retain control should in turn, provide workers with what is probably their main opportunity for direct participation and control.

NOTES

1 This was defined as 'any system of bonus payments apart from time rates' (1968, p 43).
2 More recently cited by Opsahl R L and Dunnette M D (1966). The Role of Financial Compensation in Industrial Motivation, *Psychological Bulletin*, Vol 66 No 2 pp 94–118.
3 Although intercorrelations show that railway supervisors are more like railway workers than any other group ($r = 0.90$) on the basis of these ratings, major differences can be largely attributed to hierarchical level. This holds equally true for sub-divisions according to rank within the military officers (junior and senior officers $r = 0.53$): however further analysis of officer rankings suggests that age may be an even more important factor (50+ and 20–30 age groups $r = 0.30$).
4 For a fuller discussion of this and other aspects of the Hawthorne studies, see chapter 6.
5 For some groups, more particularly craftsmen and some white collar workers, status may be an important associated variable.
6 Dalton found that those who restricted output, but who were not what he termed 'restricters' suffered from physiological stress symptoms due to the dissonance caused by the conflict between group pressures and the desire for high earnings.

CHAPTER SIX

CONTROL THROUGH SOCIAL PROCESSES

The human relations movement stressed the importance of social processes in the work environment and argued that management was most likely to be effective if it operated by taking the social system into account. In practice this meant that management had to provide an area of freedom within which the social processes could find expression. Combined with an attempt to obtain the involvement and commitment of the workforce, it was hoped that this approach, whilst satisfying the needs of the workers for some social control, would also further managerial goals. There are three main ways in which this control might operate. First, control can be exerted through the communication system both by the decision to communicate or not to communicate and also by the content of any communication. Secondly, control can be exerted as a result of the leadership style; one of the critical variables in leadership behaviour is the amount of freedom the leader gives his subordinates; the assumption of the human relations movement is that the greater the freedom, the more positive the response of the workforce. Thirdly, in certain circumstances, control can be exerted by the social group. Taking its conclusions from the Hawthorne studies, the human relations movement argued that a deliberate attempt to involve the group in a change process was the most likely way to gain acceptance of the change.

As in the previous chapter, two questions are of particular interest. When these social processes offer the worker the opportunity to exert control, does he make use of that opportunity? And if he does, does he use it to support or oppose managerial objectives? Communications, leadership style and group processes are examined in an attempt to answer these questions.

COMMUNICATIONS

Mechanic (1962) has argued that lower level participants in organizations may have no authority but they do have considerable personal power. He suggests that power is closely related to dependence and that "within organizations one makes others dependent upon him by controlling access to information, persons and instrumentalities" (1962, p 352). In the present context we are primarily concerned with information. Mechanic emphasizes the importance of commitment on the part of the workforce as a basis for ensuring that this power is used to further organizational goals. This view is supported by March and Simon (1958) who have argued that the "ease and accuracy of communication may depend upon both motivational and cognitive factors" (1958, p 28). This will be particularly critical in times of 'uncertainty absorption'. "Uncertainty absorption takes place when inferences are drawn from a body of evidence and the inferences, instead of the evidence itself, are then communicated ... Through the process of uncertainty absorption, the recipient of a communication is severely limited in his ability to judge its correctness . . . By virtue of specialization most information enters an organization at highly specific points. Direct perception of production processes is limited largely to employees in a particular operation on the production floor ... By the very nature of the communication system, a great deal of discretion and influence is exercised by those persons who are in direct contact with some part of the 'reality' that is of concern to the organization ... Because of this, uncertainty absorption is frequently used, consciously and unconsciously, as a technique for acquiring and exercising power" (1958, pp 165–166).

Evidence of attempts to exert control through the communication process is sparse, mainly because of difficulties in obtaining reliable information. Alternative perspectives on the communication process can be broadly analysed as follows:

The subordinate passing information up to management can:	– fully inform management – selectively inform management – falsely (amd knowingly) inform management – fail to inform management.
The subordinate receiving information from management can:	– choose to hear the information – choose to hear selective information – choose not to hear/understand the information.

Apart from these conscious processes, there are certain unintended alternatives such as unwittingly passing on false information. To find out whether there is any attempt to exert control either for or against managerial objectives, a controlled experiment must be conducted or a series of interviews carried out which examine the motivation of the workforce in this respect. Otherwise it would be impossible to demonstrate whether or not behaviour is merely compliant with the organization system. Equally, failure to communicate information may be due to a deliberate decision by a worker, to his apathy, to his ignorance of the need to communicate or to his perception that he would be unable to communicate. These difficulties are highlighted in a study by Mann (1953), which demonstrated how management might perceive that subordinates were deliberately failing to communicate. In contrast, the subordinates felt they were not free to communicate. For instance, while 51 per cent of the workers felt free to discuss important aspects of the job with the supervisor, 85 per cent of the supervisors considered that freedom to be available to the workers.

Roy (1952, 1953, 1955) has shown how workers may deliberately attempt to influence the passage of information. The object in this case was to persuade management that the piece-rate was too tight. The method of demonstrating this included verbal and written communication, as well as attempts to exert influence through the information management received in the form of restricted output figures and through the behaviour of the workers when management was nearby. In order to convince management that restricted behaviour was in fact genuine behaviour, and in the hope that the rate would therefore be adjusted, it was important that everyone should behave in a similar way. Therefore in this case and in the somewhat similar circumstances of the bank wiring room of the Hawthorne studies, strong group pressures were exerted to persuade everyone to conform and thereby to present management with consistent rather than conflicting information.

Muench (1960, 1963) has reported a situation in which refusal to receive communication was interpreted as a major cause of conflict. He observed the bargaining situation and noted that, although each side was quite capable of understanding the other, "the breakdown in communication was caused most often when one participant seemed unable or unwilling to understand what another participant was saying"[1] (Muench, 1963). This was interpreted as a defence mechanism which was used to protect a point of view against threatening counter arguments. By demonstrating to the participants how this defence mechanism was working, Muench claims that he was able to open up communications and virtually eliminate conflict. What this study does highlight is the rational reasons for refusing to communicate openly; both sides were using the communication process in an attempt to control and influence the bargaining situation and maintain their own position.

March and Simon (1958) suggest that non-programmable or non-routine information is often the least likely to be effectively communicated and it is therefore necessary to devise a means of passing it on. This has led to the establishment of suggestion schemes, consultative systems, briefing groups, company news-sheets and a variety of media. Most are designed to ensure that management's point of view is clearly put across to the workforce. Suggestion schemes are an exception; they exist in many organizations and operate with varying success. The study by Clarke, Fatchett and Roberts (1972) indicated the continued popularity of such schemes; 84 per cent of the respondent firms employing more than 2,000 workers had schemes, although views on their value tended to vary. Only 22·7 per cent of all respondents had a suggestion scheme with which, to a greater or lesser extent, they were satisfied. But these schemes do demonstrate that some workers have ideas to communicate and that they are often prepared to make use of this type of communication channel. Many schemes offer rewards to any individual who puts forward a worthwhile suggestion; others (see, for example, the Scanlon Plan described in Whyte, 1955, and by Industrial Relations Counsellors Inc, 1962) operate on a group basis.

Even with willing participants, accurate communication can be difficult to achieve. It is therefore relatively easy to influence the communication process and it offers undoubted scope for the individual to exert control. The likelihood that he will try to exert control is dependent upon the expectancies outlined in our theoretical framework. Since access to accurate information will often be a prerequisite to the achievement of specific goals, managers have generally favoured a limited amount of open communications at the shop-floor level as a means of furthering their own objectives. Where workers recognize this, and perceive that management interests significantly conflict with their own, they in turn will often attempt to control the information process.

LEADERSHIP STYLE

The importance of leadership style in influencing the attitudes and behaviour of subordinates has long been recognized. On the basis of interviews conducted at the Hawthorne plant of the Western Electric Company, Putnam (1930) concluded that supervision was the most important determinant of the attitudes and efficiency of the workforce. Feldman (1937) reported a field experiment which lent further support to the argument that the supervisor was a major influence on performance. More recently Likert (1961) has argued that "Widespread use of participation is one of the more important approaches employed by the high-producing managers in their efforts to get full benefit from the technical resources of the classical theories of management coupled with high levels of reinforcing motivation. This use of participation applies to all aspects of the job and work as, for example, in setting work goals and budgets, controlling costs, organizing the work etc" (1961, p 100). Since an individual's style of management can influence the amount of control which his subordinates can exercise, it is included in our review of participation.

Early experiments were able to establish the importance of supervision but failed to indicate the type of supervision which would lead to greatest job satisfaction and productivity. Lewin, Lippit and White (1939) were among the first to point to the type or style of supervision which might produce the best results. They organized 20 boys into four clubs; each club received a six-week period of autocratic leadership and then of democratic leadership. Two of the clubs also received a period of *laissez-faire* leadership. The work rate was higher under the autocratic leadership but tended to fall off when the leader was not present.[2] Under democratic leadership, the work rate was also fairly high and was maintained when the leader was absent. *Laissez-faire* leadership produced the poorest results. Democratic leadership produced the highest emotional stability and what might be termed job satisfaction.

This study contrasted democratic and authoritarian styles of leadership. Under authoritarian leadership, the leader was the sole determiner of what was to be done; his main contact with the boys occurred when he was telling them what to do. The democratic leader encouraged participation and group decision-making but provided guidance when necessary. Much subsequent research has been designed to test whether or not these are the critical dimensions. From a series of studies at Ohio University, factor analysis revealed two dimensions which were termed 'consideration' and 'initiation structure'. Consideration, sometimes referred to as employee-centred behaviour, reflects the degree to which the supervisor is warm and friendly towards his subordinates, taking their feelings into account and communicating his action to them. It differs from democratic leadership in that it is essentially one-way. The meaning of initiation structure is less clear; essentially it is a concern with production, but it has sometimes been associated with autocratic leadership. These dimensions have generated a considerable amount of research, much of it geared towards the development of measuring devices (see Fleishman, 1953; Fleishman, Harris and Burtt, 1955). Many of the findings are inconsistent and, in his review of the relevant literature, Korman (1966) commented that "there is very little evidence that leadership behavioural and/or attitudinal variation, as defined by scores on the leadership behaviour and leadership opinion questionnaire, are predictive of later effectiveness and/or satisfaction criteria" (1966, p 351). A major problem is that almost all the studies are correlational and concerned with concurrent validity. These might indicate a relationship but could not say why it existed. Korman could find no relevant experimental studies and only two small predictive field studies.

There is a wider literature on attempts to compare democratic and authoritarian leadership. Unlike the research emanating from Ohio University, these studies have tended to assume that the broad democratic-authoritarian dimension was the most significant one for leadership behaviour and have accepted the characteristics assigned to these categories by Lewin, Lippit and White (1939). Since democratic or participative leadership deliberately seeks to involve subordinates in decision-making, it is more relevant than consideration. The main approach has been to identify effective and ineffective groups and compare the leadership style of their supervisors; this typifies much of the work carried out by the Survey Research Centre at Michigan. Likert (1961) has argued that the Michigan research provides convincing evidence of the association between the democratic leadership style and high productivity and job satisfaction. Since this survey work is correlational rather than predictive, the reason for any relationship is undetermined.[3]

Even the correlational data fail to lend clearcut support to the supposed relationship between democratic supervision, productivity and satisfaction. For example, although Katz, Maccoby and Morse (1950) found that supervisors of low producing groups in an insurance company were less participative and more inclined towards close supervision, Katz, Maccoby, Gurin and Floor (1951) failed to produce similar findings for supervisors of railway maintenance teams.

One of the more sophisticated studies of this kind was conducted by Argyle, Gardner and Cioffi (1958). They compared the supervisors of 90 work groups on a number of items including five dimensions of supervisory behaviour; in particular they predicted that successful supervisors would be general in their supervision, exert low pressure and be employee-centred, democratic and non-punitive. Success was defined in terms of productivity, and satisfaction as measured by labour turnover and absenteeism. The result showed that in departments where incentive payment schemes operated, none of the supervisory dimensions was significantly related to productivity. In other departments, supervisors in charge of highly productive groups were significantly more democratic and less punitive. Combining the dimensions, a positive relation was found between an overall 'human relations' score and productivity in departments where there was no incentive bonus. Staff working under highly democratic leaders were significantly less likely to be absent but none of the dimensions was related to labour turnover. Therefore it appears from this study that democratic supervision is associated with high productivity and job satisfaction. However, the relationship appeared to be dependent upon the method of payment. The study is useful for introducing additional variables into the research programme; it is possible, for example, that items such as age, sex and method of payment could account for many of the different results of other studies. These differences are examined more fully in chapter 9.

Because their study was correlational, Argyle, Gardner and Cioffi (1958) were left with the task of deciding what could account for their results. There were three main alternatives:

1 Men work harder and are happier when they have a democratic supervisor.
2 Supervisors can afford to be more participative when they are in charge of a happy and hard-working group.
3 Certain external variables determine both the productivity and happiness of the men and the leadership style adopted by the supervisor.

The answers can only be obtained by experimentation. A number of attempts to do this have been reported. Feldman (1937) noted large differences in cost reduction among 22 separate groups of clerks after a bonus scheme had been introduced. To test the influence of the supervisors, all 22 were moved around so that those previously in charge of successful groups were now supervising the less successful groups and *vice versa*. One year later large differences in cost reduction from group to group remained, but the rank order of supervisor success was virtually unchanged, suggesting that supervision was the major variable influencing cost reduction. Unfortunately Feldman failed to produce sufficient data to back up his descriptive account.

Jackson (1953) reports a somewhat similar experiment but using attitudes rather than performance as the criteria. First he measured the attitudes of nine work groups involved in the installation and repair of telephone equipment.

The three supervisors whose behaviour was rated most favourably by subordinates were exchanged with the three who received the least favourable ratings. Later administration of the original questionnarire showed that the groups which had reacted favourably to their original supervisor reacted unfavourably to their new one. The other groups had now become more favourably disposed towards their supervisor whilst the control groups who had retained their original supervisor showed no change of attitude.

Both of these experiments demonstrate the influence of supervision on behaviour and on certain attitudes. The Lewin, Lippit and White (1939) study suggested that authoritarian supervision was most likely to have a positive impact on performance but democratic supervision was more likely to lead to positive attitudes. Morse and Reimer (1956) sought to examine this more closely among white collar employees in an insurance company. A change programme in two divisions was designed to involve employees more extensively in decision-making, whilst in a further two divisions hierarchical control was increased. This programme was continued for a year. As predicted, the autonomous group with democratic leadership showed an increase in job satisfaction in contrast to the hierarchically controlled group who showed a decrease. However, both groups showed an increase in productivity with the hierarchically controlled group showing the greater increase.

The problems of conducting experiments in the industrial environment have resulted in a number of laboratory studies. The setting throws doubt on the validity of such research; in his review of these programmes, Sales (1966) concluded that only one (Day and Hamblin 1964) showed that democratic supervision was more effective in terms of productivity, one showed that authoritarian supervision was more effective and the rest produced no significant differences.

The bulk of the evidence from the more rigorous studies suggests that hierarchical or authoritarian leadership leads to as good or possibly better performance than democratic or participative leadership, although these latter styles of leadership would seem to lead to greater job satisfaction. But even this finding is coming under attack. Rosen (1970) has reported an experiment designed to test the cause-effect relationship between supervision and performance. After studying the impact of a re-allocation of supervisors to different work groups in a furniture factory he concluded that "the data were found to be at least as friendly to the 'performance as cause' hypothesis as to the 'perceived leadership behaviour as cause' hypothesis" (1970, p 186). Some tentative support for a more complex process of interaction comes from a laboratory experiment by Lowin and Craig (1968) which indicated that changes in the performance of the group can lead to changes in the degree of democratic or authoritarian behaviour by the leader. Further research is needed and it seems likely, as Rosen argues, that a complex system model is going to be required to explain the findings. Even within the narrow perspective of leadership behaviour the work of Fiedler (1967) has emphasized the greater complexity of the issue. Briefly, he proposes that the appropriate leadership style will be a function of the nature of the task upon which the group is engaged, the power position of the leader within the organization and the relationship between the leader and his subordinates. Reddin (1970), who has been mainly concerned with higher levels of management, has also attempted a broader framework. His three-dimensional theory includes the familiar task orientation and relationships orientation and also 'effectiveness' by which he means a number of qualifying contextual factors. Like Blake (Blake and Mouton, 1964) with his 'managerial grid' Reddin is suggesting that both task and person factors should be optimized.

The democratic, participative style of leadership is said to give the workforce more freedom and more scope to become involved in decision-making and the use of initiative. Virtually none of the studies has provided details of the practical impact of participative styles of leadership.

Argyle, Gardner and Cioffi (1958) suggested that "the effect of supervision and group organization may be expected to lead to differences of the order of seven per cent to 15 per cent when these factors are changed, or when otherwise similar groups are compared" (1958, p 24). In their own investigation, which examined the possible influence of a number of factors, they concluded that supervision accounted for 18·5 per cent of the variation in output.

The workforce can generally perceive the difference between leadership styles and prefer those which allow them more freedom and participation. They do not appear to use this freedom to exert control to any significant extent, since there is no consistent relationship between leadership style and either high or low productivity. Within our theoretical framework, this could be accounted for by the perception on the part of the workers either that they have only limited control over their performance through this means or that it will not influence any significant rewards. Clearly both the informal social system and the method of payment might have an influence on behaviour in these circumstances, and it is apparent that we still do not know enough about the whole issue. This review of the literature on participative leadership, which is often used as a basis for arguments in favour of extending worker control and changing management style, is significant for indicating that its impact, in both a positive and negative sense, appears to be minimal.

THE WORK GROUP

The third approach which falls within the human relations movement, emphasizes the importance of the work group. In practice, this has led to the advocacy of work group participation often in the context of a change programme. This provides the work group with some opportunity to exert direct control over various aspects of their work situation: it is our concern in this section to examine the nature of that control and to determine how it is used.

The importance of the group has long been established by social psychologists. By testing people both individually and then as a group, Sherif (1948) was able to demonstrate that the group influenced the individual's perception of the movement of a spot of light in a darkened room. Asch (1956) demonstrated that group pressures could exert a considerable influence on an individual's perception of the size of an object.

The influence of the group will vary according to individual differences in personality. Furthermore, the influence of the group over its members is greater in circumstances when it has the power to hold on to members by affecting the attainment of desirable objectives. This power may be administered through display of friendship or through the ability to administer some sort of sanction.

In the industrial setting, a distinction can be made between the task functions of the group and its social/emotional functions. The task function relates to the formal purpose of the group, while the social/emotional function provides an outlet for affiliation needs, a means of testing out ideas and social reality, a feeling of security and power and an outlet for those who want to exercise social leadership. The high priority attached to interpersonal relations emphasizes the importance of this social/emotional function.

The interest in and study of work groups has focused largely upon change situations. This has included the study of long-term resistance to management objectives through programmes such as restriction of output or refusal to accept new working practices; the study of the use of group techniques to overcome this resistance; and the study of the role of the group in facilitating changes which affect the workforce in any way. The theoretical perspective of the human relations movement is that resistance to change is often irrational; it may well be a reaction to attempts by management to impose something new and unknown upon the workforce. The solution is to involve workers in the planning and introduction of the change so that they know what they are letting themselves in for and can obtain a sense of commitment and involvement. Whether in practice this represents a form of direct participation is open to doubt. Generally the workers are involved in decisions relating to how a change will be introduced rather than whether or not the change is acceptable; the nature of the work they will be doing after the change is seldom open to discussion. Further, if direct participation is to take place, there should be a choice of decisions and outcomes. It is unlikely that management would allow participation to continue after a group had refused a change. There may therefore be some grounds for arguing that managers have used this approach as a means of achieving their own ends. Group participation then becomes merely a means to an end rather than an end in itself.

Rommetveit (1955) has defined as norm-sending the process whereby new group norms emerge in a change situation. Three stages are involved. First, the group defines its attitudes in relation to the behaviour in question. Secondly, the degree of conformity within the group is monitored. And thirdly, the group applies pressure on its members through appropriate rewards and punishments.[4] Implicit within this is the need for the group to define the pressures for change both within the group and from outside it and to weigh up the costs of accepting or rejecting change. This presents further difficulties for group participation since it is clear that the informal group leaders or opinion leaders will have a disproportionate amount of influence.

Tannenbaum and Massarik (1961) have summarized the advantages for management which, according to the literature, will accrue if work-group participation is accepted. In fact, these arguments could be used to justify all forms of direct participation which emanate from the human relations and intrinsically motivated man perspectives. For the present, they serve as a useful check list against which the various attempts at work-group participation can be measured.

1 There should be a higher rate of output and a better quality of work.
2 There should be a reduction in labour turnover, absenteeism and lateness.
3 There should be a reduction in the number of grievances and a more peaceful union-management and subordinate-management relationship.
4 There should be a greater readiness on the part of workers to accept change.
5 There should be a greater ease in managing subordinates.
6 This approach should facilitate an improvement in the quality of management decisions.

Implicit in these assumptions is the belief that these changes are also to the good of the worker. No mention is made of passing on rewards to him. Instead it is taken for granted that his long term goals coincide with those of management and that he will benefit if the organization as a whole benefits.

Evidence on the positive impact of work-group participation overlaps, in part, with that used in support of participative leadership. Likert (1961), for example, has said that "In several studies involving widely different kinds of work . . . the loyalty of non-supervisory employees towards their workgroup and pride in its ability to produce are found to have a low positive relationship with productivity". The theme of his work constantly emphasizes the relationship between group cohesion, group morale, job satisfaction and productivity despite the rather limited support from the correlational data: in this there is a tendency to gloss over some of the many problems involved. In contrast, Tannenbaum and Massarik (1961) have described rather more explicitly the conditions under which successful participation is likely to occur. Although our concern is with work-group participation, once again many of these conditions also apply to participative leadership.

1 The group or individual must be capable of becoming psychologically involved in the relevant activities.

2 The group or individual must favour the outcome of the activity.

3 Each individual must see the relevance of the activity to himself.

4 The group or individual must be capable of self expression to their own satisfaction.

5 There must be enough time to take decisions.

6 The approach adopted must be economically sound.

7 There should be no threat of any sort to anyone's feeling of security.

8 The stability of the management – subordinate relationship must be maintained.

9 There must be adequate channels of communication.

10 The participants must be aware of the function and purpose of the enterprise.

These items are not all included on the basis of evidence of their influence; but, taken at their face value, they add up to a formidable list of constraints.

There is an extensive literature on the influence of the group in the work setting, including its influence on decision-making. Once again much of the data is correlational, leaving open the question of cause and effect. A number of studies, particularly those which use questionnaire evidence and relate freedom of decision-making to supervision run the risk of a halo effect, whereby the popular supervisor receives a high rating on almost all variables and the converse holds true for the unpopular supervisor (see, for example, Jacobson, 1951; Wickert, 1951 and Ross and Zander 1957).

The Hawthorne studies (Roethlisberger and Dickson, 1939) invariably provide a starting point in any review of relevant research. Although at least five rather separate investigations were involved, it is those in the relay assembly test room and the bank wiring observation room that have attracted most attention. The relay assembly test room experiment arose out of earlier work on the impact of changes in illumination and was an attempt to understand why performance had improved even among those whose lighting had remained unaltered. The main part of the experiment lasted for a period of two and a half years, during which a group of six girls working on a simple repetitive task of assembling small relays were carefully monitored. Most of these changes involved variations in rest pauses and hours of work. There were 13 experimental periods in all, at the end of which output had risen by approximately 30 per cent. This rate of improvement was maintained, even when the girls returned to conditions prior to the changes, with full hours and no rest pauses. Although subsequent investigations within the overall programme indicated that some of the improvement could be attributed to variations in the incentive payment scheme, the researchers eventually attributed the major improvement to social factors, in particular to the development of a cohesive informal group and to the absence of strict control and supervision. This recognition of the importance of social factors was the significant point which enabled the Hawthorne studies to be seen as a major breakthrough.

Further support for the influence of the social group came from the bank wiring observation room. Fourteen men, doing separate but somewhat interdependent tasks, were observed over six and a half months. During this time it was clear that the men were responding to group pressures to restrict output rather than to the company's incentive payment scheme. The social group used a number of sanctions such as name-calling and physical punching, as a means of exercising control; at the same time, status within the group could be enhanced by adjusting work returns either up or down to reflect a standard day to day rate of performance. The conclusion drawn from the investigation was that interpersonal relations were a more important influence on behaviour than the incentive payment scheme. While this may have been true, it would be wrong as a result to claim, as so many people have done, that social factors are more important than money. The interaction of pay, interpersonal relations and job security becomes clearer when it is known that the observation period ended because the depression resulted in the men being made redundant.

The Hawthorne studies have been turned into an important landmark and, in receiving attention, have also attracted widespread criticism. Most of this criticism has been directed at the relay assembly test room experiment. Landsberger (1958) has provided a comprehensive review of criticisms associated with both the conduct of the investigations and the interpretations of the findings. Carey (1967) has questioned the way in which certain of the results were presented and Argyle (1953) has argued that most of the increase in output can be accounted for by the replacement of the two slowest girls, the introduction of rest periods and adjustments to the incentive payment scheme. Blumberg (1968) claims that in interpreting the findings, the researchers missed the point and that the real significance of the experiment lies in its demonstration of the positive impact of participation. He considers that much of the rise in output was the result of involving the girls in discussions about the type of change that should take place and allowing their opinions to influence subsequent adjustments. In other words, Blumberg is presenting an even stronger case than the Hawthorne researchers or Mayo (1933) for the value of work-group participation.

A further series of influential studies, this time in a non-industrial setting, was conducted by Lewin (Lewin, in Maccoby, Newcomb and Hartley, 1958). These were concerned with attempts to change the eating habits of American women. He compared the effectiveness of a lecture programme and group discussions as a means of persuading the women to buy unpopular meats such as beef hearts and kidneys. The results showed that while only three per cent of those who had heard the lectures changed their eating habits, 32 per cent of those who had participated in the group discussions had done so. These findings were substantiated in later experiments by Radke and Klisurich (1947) who also examined eating habits, and by others whose concern was with behaviour in relation to breast cancer.

Moving back to the industrial context, Bavelas (French, 1950) compared methods of changing informal group norms at the Harwood garment factory. Groups of female sewing-machine operators were invited to discuss means of raising productivity and then to set higher productivity goals. Each experimental group was matched with a control group. Four months later the experimental groups displayed an average increase in output of 18 per cent whilst the control groups showed virtually no change.

In the same Harwood factory, Coch and French (1948) conducted an experiment designed to examine the influence of the group in overcoming resistance to change. Four roughly comparable groups were involved. Each was to be subjected to one of the fairly frequent changes which the nature of the product necessitated. In two experimental groups, each operator was given an opportunity to participate directly in helping to reach decisions related to the change. A third experimental group appointed representatives who helped to work out details of the change. Finally, there was a control group where the changes were introduced in the normal way, that is by means of a meeting at which the details of the changes were announced. After the changes were introduced, there were large differences in productivity levels. In the first two experimental groups, where everyone had had the opportunity to participate, it took four days to reach pre-change levels of production and the level eventually settled down 14 per cent above what it had been before the change. The third experimental group, for which the representatives had discussed the changes, reached pre-change levels after 14 days and remained at that level. The control group showed a marked drop in output; there were signs of aggression towards management and a high level of labour turnover. These problems continued until the group was broken up.

French, Israel and Ås (1960) reported an attempt to repeat this success on a Norwegian population. Nine four-man groups were involved in the change. Four of these were control groups with whom the change was introduced in the traditional way. Everyone in the other groups was involved in discussions, mainly concerned with the allocation of products to groups. Two of the groups were more fully involved in discussions of other relevant aspects of the change. After the change, all the groups returned to a similar level of production as before; the only difference was that the two experimental groups returned to this level more quickly. Also, the experimental groups displayed slightly more job satisfaction. Work group participation had led to no significant improvement in either satisfaction or productivity.

The difference between the results of these two experiments can be explained by a number of factors. First, at Harwood the groups were given some control over changes in important outcomes, and particularly over rates of pay. This was not so in the Norwegian experiment. Secondly, in Norway, memory of previous experiences indicated that a majority of the workforce felt that any increase in output would result in a cut in piece-rates. Thirdly, there were strong informal norms of negotiation through representatives on issues of this type in the Norwegian factory; these were ignored by the research team. Fourthly, the introduction of change at Harwood was dramatic and likely to heighten differences between the experimental and control groups. But the main point still obtains: that work-group change programmes are only likely to be successful if they are seen by the workforce to involve virtually no risk and if they enable the group to reach decisions about matters which they perceive to be important.

Another potential problem for the small group approach to change was highlighted by Strauss (Whyte, 1955). A recent change had meant that a team of girls who sprayed paint on dolls had the speed of their work determined by a moving belt. This resulted in low morale and a poor quality of work. In an attempt to overcome these problems, fan heaters were introduced and then the girls were allowed to set the pace of the production line. Within three weeks the girls were operating 30 to 50 per cent above the expected levels and earning more than many of the skilled workers; also, their speed was upsetting other sections of the production line. Their control was therefore arbitrarily revoked with the result that production dropped, six of the eight girls left within a month and even the foreman left after a few months.

The costs of ignoring the role of the work-group are highlighted in the studies conducted by Trist and Bamforth (1951) in the British coal mines. Traditionally, mining work was carried out, at the coal-seam, by small groups under conditions in which the group served a number of functions. Apart from their technical role, these groups consisted of people who knew and trusted each other so that they were able to depend on each other for security and comfort in a dangerous work environment. Not surprisingly these relationships often extended outside the workplace. The new longwall method ignored the importance of interpersonal relations; despite its technical superiority, it therefore failed to result in higher productivity. The Tavistock Institute research team was able to redress this situation by taking account of both the technical and social requirements within their socio-technical systems approach.

The weight of evidence indicates that work-group participation can lead to positive improvements in performance and job satisfaction. The success of the approach is dependent on a number of factors. Obviously it can only be used where management feels that the technical system permits the work-group a certain area of freedom. Consistent with our model of motivation, the outcomes which can be affected by work-group decisions must be perceived as important and the possible gains which may accrue to the workforce must outweigh any expected losses. A comparison of the more and less successful change programmes again highlights the significance of pay, interpersonal relations and job security. In fact the success or failure of the programmes reported in the literature can be explained in terms of the criteria listed by Tannenbaum and Massarik and outlined earlier in this chapter.

Although the majority of reported studies indicate that group involvement in change produces positive results in terms of both performance and job satisfaction, we remain sceptical about the long-term success of this strategy unless the workers are provided with a rather more permanent form of control. Autonomous work groups represent one attempt to achieve this. In any case, the actual amount of control provided by work group participation can be questioned; and it may be more legitimate to regard it as a means of facilitating the attainment of managerial goals in circumstances where the workers feel that these goals do not conflict with their own objectives. As we emphasized earlier, the conditions for participation in its fullest sense could only exist if management accepted the right of the work-group to veto changes. It is the absence of any awareness of this which has led some observers (see, for example, Mills, 1948; Child, 1969) to argue that the human relations movement is essentially manipulative.

Summary

This chapter has examined the scope and impact of the direct participation permitted by the communication system, by participative leadership and by work-group participation. The communication system offers the worker control over whether or not to communicate and what to communicate. Participative leadership can offer the worker more freedom to express opinions and influence certain decisions and thereby exert control. Finally the work-group can exert control when it is involved in decisions, particularly in the context of a change programme. Although in theory each of these conditions provides subordinates with the opportunity to exert control, in practice it is doubtful how far management will permit participative leadership and work-group participation to continue where the worker uses this control to oppose managerial goals. The result, therefore, may often be a form of pseudo-participation. Another problem is that only a limited amount of evidence derived from satisfactory experimental conditions is available; what there is supports the argument that workers will only use this control to any significant extent when they believe it will affect important outcomes. If so, they are most likely to seek to exert control through work-group participation, usually where a change programme of some sort is involved.

NOTES

1 Quotation from a paper The Resolution of Conflict in Union-Management Relationships, read by Muench at the American Psychological Association, 1964 and quoted in R Stagner and H Rosen (1965). *The Psychology of Union-Management Relations*, London; Tavistock.

2 It is difficult to evaluate this study since many of the criteria were rather doubtful. Those under autocratic supervision spent 74 per cent of their time working compared with 50 per cent of the time by those under democratic leadership. However, as Sales (1966) pointed out "no objective measure of productivity is reported by the authors, and therefore it is impossible to determine accurately which of the two styles evoked the higher production" (1966, p 278).

3 A correlational study can show that a relationship exists between two sets of factors. It cannot provide a causal explanation of why it exists. A predictive study, as its name implies, sets out to predict that a specified variable will interact with another to produce certain results. It usually requires measures of behaviour before and after an experimental variable, such as a change in leadership, has been introduced and while other factors are held constant. Because of these rigorous requirements, it is difficult to carry out these studies in real life.

4 Of course, new group norms can also be internalized as a result of sanctions imposed by those external to the group.

CHAPTER SEVEN

WORKER PARTICIPATION THROUGH JOB ENRICHMENT

This chapter is divided into two sections; the first examines the theories associated with the intrinsically-motivated man school. In particular, Herzberg's two-factor theory of motivation is critically evaluated and attempts to replicate it are discussed. The second section examines the impact of job enrichment, concentrating on its application to blue-collar workers.

(i) THE CONCEPT OF JOB ENRICHMENT

The concepts associated with intrinsically-motivated man originated in the writings of Maslow (1943) and were adapted for industry by McGregor (1960), with his advocacy of practices associated with Theory Y, and by Herzberg (Herzberg, Mausner and Snyderman, 1959) with his two-factory theory. Closely associated approaches were developed by a number of organization development theorists such as Bennis (1966) Schein (Schein and Bennis, 1965) and Blake (Blake and Mouton, 1964) and by those who adopted a socio-technical systems perspective (see, for example, Trist *et al*, 1963; Emery and Thorsrud, 1969). Although each of these approaches starts from a rather different point, they all have something in common to say about job design, by advocating what is variously described as job enrichment, job enlargement, work-structuring, group technology or autonomous work grouping.

Much of the applied work associated with this general perspective has been carried out with executive and professional groups rather than with blue-collar workers and much of it has been geared to meet the needs of management education and development. For example, the main impact of McGregor's ideas has been on the reform of appraisal systems and the development of management by objectives; and organization development has been mainly, though not exclusively, synonymous with management development. The applied techniques which have most relevance for blue-collar workers stem from the socio-technical systems approach and from the ideas of Herzberg. We shall have more to say about the impact of the socio-technical systems approach later in the chapter. By and large, management has been initially attracted by the apparently more straightforward ideas of Herzberg and has tended to concentrate on the concept of job enrichment.

Job enrichment is defined as the process whereby the interest and involvement in a job is increased by building into it more opportunity for achievement, responsibility and autonomy. Although there has been some confusion of terms, it is, in theory at least, quite distinct from job enlargement, which is the process of introducing more variety into the job by increasing the number of different tasks that have to be performed. At this stage it is also helpful to distinguish a third approach, job rotation, which entails moving from one job or task to another on a pre-determined rota basis. Since all these tasks may be equally boring and routine, its advantage lies in the variety which it injects. The satisfaction this engenders by this is likely to be short-lived unless the rotation leads to the existence of a larger and more meaningful job, in which case it is closer to job enlargement. Work-structuring, autonomous work groups and the like owe more to the socio-technical systems approach; they generally have similar aims to job enrichment but focus upon the work group rather than the individual; they also tend to be more aware of the technological constraints. Although in theory it is possible to draw a distinction between these terms, in practice they are sometimes used interchangeably. In the present context, job enrichment has the most fully developed theoretical antecedents; this, coupled with its appeal to management, singles it out for attention and we turn next to a fairly detailed examination of Herzberg's two-factor theory on which it is largely based.

HERZBERG'S ORIGINAL CONTRIBUTION

In 1957, Herzberg and his associates published a review of the literature which had accumulated over the last 50 years on job attitudes and in particular on job satisfaction and its relation to productivity (Herzberg, *et al*, 1957). Their conclusions supported the evidence cited in the last chapter which indicated that there was no clearcut relation between job satisfaction and productivity. This finding constituted a blow to those advocates of the human relations movement who argued, at least by implication, that a satisfied worker would also be a productive worker. The one finding that did emerge with consistency was that different job factors were cited when people were asked what made them satisfied with their work and what made them dissatisfied.

A method of investigation was devised to examine this more closely and then tested on approximately 200 engineers and accountants working in and around Pittsburgh. The two-factor or motivator-hygiene theory emerged from this research. It stated that job satisfaction was made up of two quite separate components; first there were the hygiene factors which, if absent, led to dissatisfaction but which, if present in a job, merely led to a state of no dissatisfaction and not to a positive feeling of satisfaction. These included pay, supervision, company policy and other extrinsic factors (see Figure 3). Secondly, there were the motivator factors, the absence of which prevented satisfaction though it did not necessarily lead to active dissatisfaction but which, when present, led to positive satisfaction. The motivator factors included the intrinsic aspects of the job such as achievement, responsibility and the nature of the work itself. The content analysis of the questionnaire responses suggested that the motivator factors were often associated with times of individual effort and productivity. The implication was that, to obtain a combination of job satisfaction and productivity, the needs of the individual should be taken into account by building more motivator factors into the job and by moving away from the traditional emphasis on the hygiene factors. This process of 'enrichment' often required an individual to take on certain responsibilities which traditionally had been the prerogative of management. In this way it gave the worker more control and was a form of direct participation: for this reason it justifies our concern. Nevertheless Herzberg did not see job enrichment as a totally participative process: "Although there is no room for individual participation in the setting of goals, it is certainly possible that the ways in which these goals are to be reached can be left to the judgement of the individuals. . . . This is a reasonable solution to the problem of

Figure 3

MOTIVATOR AND HYGIENE FACTORS

Motivator Factors	Hygiene Factors
Achievement	Salary
Recognition	Interpersonal relations with subordinates
Work itself	Interpersonal relations with peers
Responsibility	Interpersonal relations with superiors
Advancement	Supervision – technical
Possibility of growth	Company policy and administration
	Working conditions
	Personal life
	Status
	Job security

motivation, more reasonable than the usual formulation of participation. To expect individuals at lower levels in an organization to exercise control over the establishment of over-all goals is unrealistic" (Herzberg, Mausner and Snyderman, 1959, pp 136–137). This comment must cast doubt upon the truly participative nature of job enrichment. At the same time, it is likely to be reassuring to any managers who might see job enrichment as a threat to their control and authority.

CRITICISMS OF THE THEORY AND OF THE ORIGINAL RESEARCH

Before looking at the evidence, it is important to recognize that the theory has been strongly criticized. This may not be of crucial importance if its application is an undoubted success, but this has not so far been the case. Since Herzberg has subsequently attached considerable significance to his original approach, the next section reviews some of the main criticisms.

1 *Criticisms of the methodology*

The method of questioning devised by Herzberg, Mausner and Snyderman for use in their main study was derived from Flanagan's (1954) critical incident technique. Instead of asking about critical incidents associated with events, they asked for critical incidents associated with feelings. In fact, respondents were asked to think about times when they felt particularly bad or particularly good at work. This encourages the intrusion of subjective feelings, since any particularly emotional event is likely to be coloured by the emotions involved. Vroom (1964) has argued that "it is still possible that obtained differences between stated sources of satisfaction and dissatisfaction stem from defensive processes within the individual respondent. Persons may be more likely to attribute the causes of satisfaction to their own achievements and accomplishments on the job. On the other hand, they may be more likely to attribute their dissatisfaction, not to personal inadequacies or deficiencies, but to factors in the work environment, ie the obstacles presented by company policies or supervisors" (1964, p 129).

Partial support for this hypothesis has been provided by Guest (in press) who found a tendency among a group of 40 dock workers to project the blame or report inaccurately when describing times when they felt particularly dissatisfied. This did not extend to times when they felt satisfied. The use of the critical incident technique in this context has also been criticized because it provides only a narrow picture of an individual's feelings and motives. For example, Hinton (1968) examined the reliability of the approach by asking subjects to cite an incident on one occasion and then asking them to cite another one six weeks later. He found considerable variation in the factors mentioned and, in particular, a tendency to switch readily from motivators to hygiene factors or *vice versa*.

Criticism has been aimed not only at the use of the critical incident technique but also at the nature of the key questions. Some people have difficulty recalling times when they felt particularly good or bad; others may be unable to say why they felt as they did. Herzberg, Mausner and Snyderman were aware of this and admit that they ran into difficulties when they tried out the approach on clerical and production workers. For this reason they concentrated, in their initial study, on more articulate groups of accountants and engineers.

This initial focus upon professional workers has led to criticisms of the sample. In his subsequent book, Herzberg (1966) quoted a number of studies, some with blue-collar workers, which lent general support to his theory; nevertheless a question mark remains over how the theory would have looked had the original research been based on blue-collar workers.

Other criticisms of the methodology include the argument put forward by House and Wigdor (1967) that the coding system used to classify the incidents is open to interpretation by the coder which may have allowed an inadvertent bias to creep in. Wall and Stephenson (1971) have suggested that the coding system is inadequate for certain kinds of responses. They cite the ambiguity caused by someone who reported a 'good' event which was due to a lack of responsibility.

2 Criticisms of the findings of the original studies

Interpretation of the original findings and the subsequent evidence cited in support by Herzberg is confused by ambiguity about the type of hypotheses that can be derived from the theory. Wall and Stephenson (1971) have suggested that there are two main hypotheses:

"1 In satisfied sequences: motivators occur more frequently than hygiene factors. In dissatisfied sequences: hygiene factors occur more frequently than motivators."

House and Wigdor's (1967) analysis of Herzberg's evidence shows that motivators took up five of the first nine places in a rank order of dissatisfiers.

"2 Motivators occur more frequently in satisfied as opposed to dissatisfied sequences. Hygiene factors occur more frequently in dissatisfied as opposed to satisfied sequences" (Wall and Stephenson, 1971, p 46).

Herzberg, Mausner and Snyderman (1959) recognized the weaknesses of the first interpretation and modified their original hypothesis to say that "a better statement of the hypothesis would be that the satisfier factors are much more likely to increase job satisfaction than they would be to decrease job satisfaction" (1959, p 80). The evidence does not fully support Wall and Stephenson's second hypothesis. For example, in the original study, 'possibility of growth' was more often cited as a source of dissatisfaction than of satisfaction and 'interpersonal relations with subordinates', a hygiene factor, was more often cited as a source of satisfaction.

An even more rigorous analysis was carried out by King (1970) who isolated five interpretations of the theory. His review of all the available studies led him to the conclusion that there was no firm support for any of the interpretations. Because of a concern about the methodology, he based his conclusion on the principle of multiple operationalism which states that a hypothesis is validated if and only if it is supported by two or more different methods of testing it, where each method may contain specific weaknesses but where a combination of methods eliminates all the weaknesses (Webb *et al*, 1966). If this were discounted, there would be some support for the general hypothesis that "all motivators combined contribute more to job satisfaction than to job dissatisfaction and all hygienes combined contribute more to dissatisfaction than satisfaction" (King, 1970, p 19).

This brief review is sufficient to indicate that it is doubtful whether the available evidence supports the two-factor theory. The weakness of the theory does not necessarily invalidate the principles of job enrichment. Nevertheless, doubts about the validity of the theory could be of crucial importance in interpreting the success or failure of attempts to put it into practice through job enrichment programmes.

TWO-FACTOR THEORY AND BLUE-COLLAR WORKERS

In his review of this approach to motivation, Vroom's plea was for "further research using the same methods on a large number of different populations" (Vroom, 1964, p 129). A number of replications appeared in Herzberg's later book (Herzberg, 1966): unfortunately many of these dealt with supervisory, managerial or professional staff, although there were some exceptions. Herzberg cites the work of Scott Myers (1964) at Texas Instruments where 75 hourly-paid male technicians and 52 hourly-paid female assembly workers provided results which confirmed the basic theory. A study by Anderson (Herzberg, 1966, p 116) ran into difficulty because a third could not think of a time when they had felt exceptionally good; however the evidence he obtained from 35 unskilled hospital workers and 31 maintenance engineers supported the theory. Further support came from a replication by Gendel (Herzberg, 1966, p 117) on 119 housekeeping workers.

A number of other studies have provided mixed evidence. They are not considered here because they did not use Herzberg's methodology (for a fuller review see House and Wigdor (1967), Whitsett and Winslow (1967), King (1970) and Wall and Stephenson (1971)). The limited available data on American blue-collar workers provides persuasive evidence for the theory. These results may be partly a function of the American value-system which places a high premium on success and advancement at work. In other cultures the results might be rather different because of alternative value systems. The evidence cited by Herzberg dealing with Finnish supervisors and Hungarian engineers supports the theory but is not derived from blue-collar workers. Finally, support for the theory even in America is partly contingent upon the use of the original methodology; more conventional measures of job satisfaction are less likely to replicate the findings.

EVIDENCE FROM THE UNITED KINGDOM

Despite extensive discussion of the two-factor theory and of the application of job enrichment in the United Kingdom, little work has been reported which seeks to test directly the soundness of the two-factor theory as a valid approach to motivation. Many of the purported tests fail to use the original methodology: therefore, despite the principle of multiple operationalism, this severely limits their value.

Typical of partial tests of the theory is the work of Gill (Mackenzie Davey *et al*, 1970) who initially interviewed factory workers, asked them what satisfied them most and least about working at the particular factory, and adapted the responses into a questionnaire which covered items which were similar to Herzberg's factors. The two-factor theory was tested through the assumption that motivators would be the main sources of satisfaction and would contribute to satisfaction rather than to dissatisfaction. This broadly held true; items that came out at the top of the list were responsibility, achievement and the work itself, followed by supervision and the working conditions. Recognition and advancement were both major sources of dissatisfaction with recognition receiving more unfavourable than favourable comments.

Another variation on Herzberg's method was used by Guest on railway station workers: initial interviews had suggested that the original key questions were not meaningful to a number of the workers. Therefore instead of asking respondents to "think of a time when you felt good" the question was "think of the job or type of work which you most (least) enjoyed and explain why". Among the 175 railmen in the sample, a small majority cited hygiene factors rather than motivators as sources of satisfaction. Hygiene factors very clearly predominated as explanations for least liked jobs. However, among 42 railway clerical workers, motivators provided the majority of reasons for liking particular jobs and also for disliking jobs. In the latter context boredom or work that was too simple were the major sources of dissatisfaction.

Wall, Stephenson and Skidmore (1971) tested the hypothesis that the nature of an individual's response to questions such as those posed by Herzberg will be determined by his need for social approval. In their initial study, 14 job applicants and 14 members of a similarly constituted control group of current employees were asked questions similar to those in the original Herzberg study. The job applicants, who were supposedly highly ego-involved, gave responses which fitted closely with the two-factor theory. Current employees displayed a rather different pattern: motivator and hygiene factors were both equally important in 'feel good' incidents whilst hygiene factors still remained more frequently associated with 'feel bad' incidents. Subsequent work on a larger sample also indicated that the need for social approval was the crucial factor in determining the nature of the response. Unfortunately this interpretation raises as many questions as it answers. The researchers seem to assume that all those who have fitted into the two-factor patterns have a high need for social approval, and that other researchers failed to get round this problem by putting those interviewed entirely at ease. They also assume that their measure of social approval is valid and, perhaps most dubious of all, that the two-factor responses correspond to a pattern of socially approved responses that are common across several cultures and job levels. It is also unfortunate, in the present context, that this in itself does not provide us with a deeper understanding of the validity of the motivational assumptions derived from the two-factor theory. Nevertheless, taken at their face value, these findings do not disprove the theory; rather they leave it not proven.

In an attempt to test several of the more controversial aspects of the two-factor theory, Guest (in press) repeated the original sequence of questions and then asked a series of further related questions to a sample of 40 dock workers, 43 dock supervisors and 23 dock managers. On the crucial question of 'feel good' and 'feel bad' incidents, the total sample fitted broadly into the Herzberg pattern. Although the size of these sub-samples was rather too small to derive conclusions with confidence about individual factors, the general trend of motivator and hygiene factors was quite clear. Among the 40 dockers, hygiene factors constituted the bulk of both 'feel good' and 'feel bad' incidents. The results for the 43 supervisors corresponded broadly with Herzberg's results, but for the 23 managers motivator factors made up the majority of both 'feel good' and 'feel bad' incidents. Close examination of these results indicates that they fit easily into Maslow's hierarchy. The results could also be explained in terms of differing orientations to work; whilst the dockers emphasize extrinsic factors managers, and to a slightly lesser extent supervisors, tend to stress intrinsic job factors and to display the conventional middle-class values.

Another almost direct replication was conducted by Daniel (1970), who asked 50 process operators in a modern plant in the petro-chemicals industry slightly adapted questions about times when they felt good and bad. His results supported Herzberg strongly; 70 per cent of 'feel good' incidents related to achievement, 18 per cent to recognition, 8 per cent to advancement and 6 per cent to various hygiene factors. A further 14 per cent could think of nothing (the figures add up to over 100 per cent since some people cited more than one factor). These results were quite different from those obtained with dock workers; some of the possible reasons for this are explored later.

One of the distinctive elements of the philosophy of intrinsically motivated man is that it has been derived from psychological research. In the last few pages we have traced the evolution of the two-factor theory and of research which has attempted to assess its validity. It appears that most of the American work using the original interview schedule has supported the theory. In the United Kingdom the picture is different; little research has been reported and what has does not clearly support the theory at the level of the blue-collar worker. Therefore those who are attempting to introduce job enrichment for their workforce are doing so largely as an act of faith, because it seems intuitively close to common sense or because the reports they have read have led them to believe that it works. Alternatively they are making deductions from non-comparable evidence on samples from the American culture and from a predominantly professional and managerial level.

(ii) THE IMPACT OF JOB ENRICHMENT AS A FORM OF CONTROL

Herzberg's original thesis was that a link would be detected between factors, attitudes and effects. In other words, 'feel good' events would be associated with, and instrumental in leading to, high performance. The evidence from his original study provided some support for this but little research has subsequently been conducted on this part of the theory. Herzberg has argued strongly that the two-factor theory leads to the recommendation that jobs should be re-designed to build in the motivators – in other words, jobs should be enriched.

As we have already stressed, it is possible to advocate job enrichment without supporting the two factor theory. The variant of autonomous work groups, for example, has been derived from the socio-technical systems concept. Offering an industrial point of view, a senior personnel manager, speaking at an Industrial Society conference on the subject, suggested that "the technique of job enrichment is not particularly revolutionary and some would argue that it is only codifying something that the good manager should do in the normal course of events" (reported in the *Financial Times*, 17.4.70). Another managerial viewpoint has been emphasized by those companies who have argued that in the face of rising absenteeism and labour turnover and changing employee expectations, job enrichment makes sound economic sense. Finally the debate on the quality of working life has resulted in reports sponsored by the European Economic Community [EEC] and the British Government, both of which strongly advocate investment in this area.

This section examines some of the evidence with the particular objectives of determining whether or not job enrichment gives the worker more control; whether or not it has any impact; and if it does, to what this impact can be attributed.

EVIDENCE FROM THE UNITED KINGDOM

An early series of case studies, which were to receive wide publicity, were carried out at ICI (Paul and Robertson, 1969, 1970). These used an experimental approach, with control groups and a careful attempt to hold other factors constant. A variety of performance and attitude criteria were used as before and after measures. The crucial weakness, particularly for our present purposes, is the sample. After the earlier criticism of Herzberg's theory on the grounds that it was derived from a white-collar sample, it is perhaps unfortunate that the ICI studies were carried out on groups of sales representatives, design engineers, experimental officers, draughtsmen and foremen, with only minor attention to shop floor workers. Although close examination of these studies reveals certain methodological weaknesses, particularly in the nature of the criteria used to assess the changes, most of them do point towards some positive effects of job enrichment.

Job Enrichment Case Study

The experiment with the foremen can serve as an illustration of the issues involved. In fact, two separate groups of foremen, one at ICI and the other at Imperial Metal Industries (IMI) constituted the sample.

The changes

The technical changes included:

> *production foremen were authorized to modify loading and sequencing schedules*
>
> *engineering foremen were given more control of preventitive maintenance*
>
> *all foremen were assigned projects and resources were made available*
>
> *they were given more on the job responsibility*
>
> *they were invited to write monthly reports*
>
> *more recognition was given for achievement of targets.*

Financial changes included:

> *engineering foremen were given some budgetary control*
>
> *production foremen made decisions on non-standard payments.*

Managerial changes included:

> *production foremen were given authority to select candidates*
>
> *foremen were given complete disciplinary authority, except for dismissal*
>
> *they were given formal responsibility for assessment, training and development of subordinates*
>
> *engineering foremen were more involved in joint consultation and negotiation.*

The results:

1 *Production foremen recruited nearly 100 men in six months. These recruits were rated as higher calibre than those previously selected. This also made the foremen aware of the need to fit people into appropriate work groups.*

2 *The production foremen handled the training effectively and reduced the number of men who could not do another man's job. Meanwhile there was no improvement in the control group.*

3 *Foremen accepted disciplinary authority and short-term stoppages were reduced. The number of repeated offences by those with a poor disciplinary record declined.*

4 *Foremen appeared to step up the consultation and negotiation processes and to handle them as effectively as management.*

5 *The projects demonstrated that foremen could make a contribution through their experience and expertise. The three which could be financially costed produced total savings of more than £50,000 per annum.*

6 *Foremen's budgetary control was at least as effective as management's.*

7 *The end of year appraisals of engineering foremen in the experimental group were markedly better than those in the control group.*

8 *Job satisfaction increased rather more amongst the experimental group than amongst the control group.*

The foremen in this case study were given increased control in a number of areas: the great majority accepted this control and used it in a manner compatible with managerial goals. Those who failed to identify so strongly with management were less willing to accept all the changes. For example, "A few of the longer service production foremen in one unit seemed reluctant to take the severer forms of disciplinary action" (Paul and Robertson, 1969, p 131).

Alongside these experiments on white-collar staff, two attempts were made to introduce job enrichment on the shop floor. It proved impossible to introduce control groups and it was reported that internal policies made the conditions unfavourable. Whatever the reason, these studies, one in ICI, the other in IMI were not successful.

The first experiment involved toolsetters. The quality of the product in question was often unsatisfactory; this was frequently due to machine faults rather than human error. These were dealt with by the toolsetter who could be summoned by the operator. To make the toolsetter more responsible for quality and efficiency, one toolsetter was made responsible for the efficiency of the equipment of the unit and for the quality of the unit's production. Two men were in the experimental and two in the control group. Unfortunately, the control group spontaneously 'enriched' their own jobs; furthermore some of the criteria were unreliable. However, on the key criterion of the quality of work there was no improvement.

The second study involved 16 process operators. The changes introduced to enrich their jobs were as follows: they were allowed to fix their own breaks and arrange cover; they took decisions about dealing with batches of work; they were encouraged to raise maintenance needs, and they were made responsible for certain 'efficiencies'. The first three changes worked reasonably well, although the supervisors soon regained control of the maintenance requests. The calculations associated with the plant efficiencies were seen as a chore and eventuallly had to be abandoned. On the available criteria, the results showed a clear deterioration in performance. This was probably partly due to other problems in the plant, including a dramatic increase in labour turnover.

Our motivational framework would predict that these workers might accept the added responsibility if they saw certain benefits accruing, but they did not appear to have accepted responsibility as an end in itself. They therefore organized cover for breaks but refused to do the extra work associated with plant efficiencies. Again, these results would seem to emphasize the importance of job level, and associated attitudes in determining the reaction to job enrichment.

158

The experiments conducted by Paul and Robertson (ICI, 1970) were designed partly to give impetus to the personnel policies of ICI, which were reflected in two important programmes, the weekly staff agreement and the staff development programme. Both were productivity agreements in which higher productivity was, to a large extent, negotiated locally and sought mainly through changes in job design akin to job enrichment or job enlargement. An increase in earnings constituted an important part of the agreement. But this means that objectively it becomes virtually impossible to determine the reasons why changes have occurred: it may be the job design, it may be the pay. More probably it is a combination of both.

One review of these practical applications in the Petrochemical Division of ICI suggested that "By involving the staff in studies of their own work, increases in effectiveness of well in excess of 25 per cent have been achieved through the elimination of unnecessary work, better organization and planning, better methods and equipment" (Mangham, Shaw and Wilson, 1971, p 90). Evaluating the staff development programme, the same article reported that "Despite the somewhat patchy progress, the programme had started to show a clear profit within 18 months, and this does not allow for the many indirect savings and less tangible gains . . . and this enrichment of jobs and reduction in supervision has been a constant theme. Almost a quarter of the division's staff have so far had their jobs upgraded as a result of the programme" (1971, p 91). This reflected satisfaction on the part of management and a financial gain for a quarter of the workforce.

A further analysis of the impact of the productivity agreement at an ICI plant is provided by Cotgrove, Dunham and Vamplew (1971). They interviewed a sample of 60 workers in a nylon spinning factory to evaluate their reaction to various changes. "A major objective of this agreement was to achieve a significant change in labour relations" (1971, p 137). All the workers were given staff status and a number of changes in the job content were introduced. The operatives were involved in the process of change – this was seen as a crucial step. The value of this approach to job design can be seen in the comments which demonstrate that "the initial attraction was increased pay. Yet once the involvement discussions were under way, their latent interest in the job itself emerged" (1971, p 134).

To produce improved labour relations, bonus payments were abolished and an average pay increase of £3 per week was allowed within the new system of grading. The changes in job content were limited by the technology: "The gains were real. But they were also limited. The main result was the reduction in boredom rather than any increase in the intrinsic interest in the job . . . There was less hanging about and the work did make better use of abilities. There was a greater feeling of being in control" (1971, p 134). It was accepted that the changes represented job enlargement rather than job enrichment.

These various changes produced some clear cut results. In terms of productivity, output went up by 20 per cent whilst the workforce was reduced by 24 per cent. Despite an increase in machinery there was a 15 per cent reduction in maintenance staff. Labour turnover was reduced but absenteeism went up a little probably as a result of improved sickness benefits accompanying staff status. The efficiency of the conversion of polymer to yarn increased as did the machine utilization, though both of these could be partly attributed to other factors. Just over 63 per cent said they were happier or much happier as a result of the changes; 25 per cent felt no different but no one was less happy.

A somewhat similar exercise conducted with production workers in a modern, semi-automated petro-chemical works is reported by Daniel (1970). Before the changes were introduced the job had a high level of responsibility but once learnt it could become boring.

The productivity agreement "sought chiefly a reduction in manning; more flexibility among operators so that they would carry out a wider range and level of tasks over a broader span of the process, and including some simple maintenance tasks; a simplification of the grading system . . . ; a slight reduction in the seniority rules; and a stable 40-hour week with no overtime or additional payments" (1970, p 51). In return pay increases of £4-£6 per week were given and conditions of employment similar to those for salaried staff. Once again, there was a pay increase and also clear evidence of job enrichment and job enlargement.

Although there was strong hostility to these changes when they were negotiated, interviews conducted nine months later showed that 65 per cent were in favour of them and only 25 per cent against them; 68 per cent cited increased job satisfaction and interest as a reason for favouring the agreement; 30 per cent cited pay and 26 per cent the conditions of employment. Those who opposed it cited fears of redundancy, too little money and anxieties about the level of safety and lack of training. Once again the majority of the workforce held a favourable attitude towards the changes in job design.

A number of the better known United Kingdom job enrichment programmes such as those at ICI and Shell, have been based on a productivity deal. Others have usually taken place in response to a specific management problem, and interest in job enrichment as a motivational technique was seldom the starting point. Few have produced anything more than subjective evidence of success or failure. A number of the better known studies have been described by King Taylor (1972) whose primary purpose was to show what job enrichment is and how it can be of value to management. Most of the accounts she provides are anecdotal, although in some she has cited more concrete evidence. Two brief examples can illustrate this. At one company each worker was given the complete job of assembling and inspecting gas convectors where previously there had been a nine-man production line and inspectors. Initially this ran into difficulty because associated changes in payment meant that some workers would be earning less. Even so, quality apparently improved by 200 per cent and absenteeism dropped from six per cent to one per cent. Having sorted out the payment issue there was a general rise in productivity of 10 per cent and wages went up by eight per cent. At Mercury House, labour turnover prompted management to give secretaries and clerks greater responsibility. As a result labour turnover fell by 25 per cent and managers and editorial staff reported that they had more time to cover important aspects of their work.

EVIDENCE FROM EUROPE

Along with ICI and American Telephone and Telegraph, Philips were one of the first companies to experiment with job design and motivation. Their main concern has been with what they call work structuring or vertical job-enlargement. In practice this means re-organizing a production department from the bottom up, taking account of the needs and abilities of the workforce. In conception, more is owed to socio-technical systems theory than to the two-factor theory. A number of these early localized experiments were written up, primarily as a basis for internal discussion (Philips, 1969). One involved changes in an electrical assembly task whereby assembly lines of 11 or 22 people were replaced by groups of three. "This new assembly method created possibilities for a more pleasant lay-out, individual quality feedback, a better team spirit and much greater resilience with regard to absenteeism and turnover" (1969, p 33). The results were an improvement in quality, a three per cent rise in output and a decrease in labour turnover and absenteeism. Instead of having a foreman and four chargehands, each of whom supervised about 20 people, assembly-bosses, responsible for about 30 people, were introduced. The short-term costs of the change were considerable, since re-tooling and increased training were required. Despite this, it was one of the more successful experiments; the others reported alongside it tended to highlight the problems of carrying out changes in job design rather than the benefits which might accrue.

Interest in the motivational implications of job design was also expressed at an early stage in Scandinavia. In Norway, for example, Emery and Thorsrud (1969) had concluded that worker participation at board level produced no real sense of involvement among the workers and, if they wanted it to succeed, management should develop participation at the more meaningful level of the worker's job.

Despite a number of well-publicized expressions of interest in job enrichment and autonomous work groups, it seems that in the 1960s there was far more talk than action. This was confirmed by Wilkinson (1971), who set out "to collect evidence on the *results* of redesigning work with a view to achieving improved motivation" (1970, p 1). He attempted to make contact with all the organizations in Europe which had been involved in relevant exercises. He discovered that "very few companies in Europe indeed have carried out work of this kind on a significant scale or have been involved for more than 12–18 months; the fact is that the three large companies in the world who for the past four or five years have been receiving wide publicity for their experiments in job enrichment and work structuring are virtually the only companies where large numbers of employees have been involved in this kind of work over a fairly long period" (1970, p 2). In all, he found 24 companies which were adopting motivational strategies of job design and examined 32 applications. These were in Norway, Sweden, Denmark, the Netherlands and the United Kingdom. Since only two companies were found in the United Kingdom, this confirms that the approach had received a disproportionate amount of publicity. It must be emphasized that, for our present purposes, we are also interested in any changes in job design which result in giving the worker the opportunity to exercise greater control, even though this may not have originated in a particular motivational strategy.

163

Wilkinson was concerned with results in terms of productivity and found that while "many companies were convinced that the experiments had led to improvements in productivity of some kind" . . . "there was an almost universal absence of 'hard' measurement" (1970, p 18). Companies justified this either by saying that the pressures towards industrial democracy were the prime reasons for undertaking the exercises or by saying there was little point in measuring the results because, whatever they showed, the changes were irreversible. Nevertheless, he concluded that in his judgement 14 of the 21 exercises which had been in progress long enough to justify an evaluation could be considered successful in terms of the profits/costs ratio.

It proved virtually impossible to isolate specific criteria of success or failure. It was apparent that the manner in which any changes in job design were introduced was just as important as the nature of the changes themselves. This strongly suggests that a number of factors were at work. "No case was found where 'motivational job-and-organization-design' in any 'pure' form had made any significant difference; in fact, the impression was that it required substantial support from some more concrete, familiar kind of event" (1970, p 76). This tends to run counter to the ICI experiments of Paul and Robertson (1970) in which all hygiene factors were held constant. The great majority of employees covered in the Wilkinson study were blue-collar staff whereas all those involved in the successful Paul/Robertson experiments were white-collar staff of one sort or another.

Although reluctant to discuss the impact of any changes, Wilkinson does describe the type of changes that occurred. For example:

"Greatly increased output per man, leading to opportunity to lower prices, thereby capturing a greatly increased share of the market; this led in turn to expansion of the company giving further benefits of scale".

"Increased output, coupled with reduced absence and

turnover and a reduction in maintenance staff (1971, p 71).

Other changes included achievement of objectives with a smaller or less skilled workforce, increased sales, reduction in waste and a reduction in maintenance costs.

Quite apart from changes in productivity, 22 of the applications claimed a change in attitude. This presumably means an increase in job satisfaction and greater identification with the company. Nine of the 16 'successful' applications reported a change of attitude; this does not preclude the existence of such a change in the other successful applications. What it may mean is that, like Wilkinson, those concerned regarded attitude change merely as a first step on the path to the more significant changes in productivity.

In the early 1970s there appears to have been a more rapid growth in the number of organizations taking active steps to re-structure jobs and interest has also been shown at the national level. Despite the widening debate on the quality of working life, the reasons for this activity are primarily economic and the motivation and well-being of the workforce has remained of secondary importance. The policy of Volvo is typical of this approach – a company which has received extensive publicity on account of plans for a new production plant based on the socio-technical principle of autonomous work groups. One of the main reasons for deciding to set up this new type of plant was that the Swedish workforce was no longer willing to accept work on a traditional car production line and this was reflected in the high levels of labour turnover and absenteeism.

EVIDENCE FROM THE UNITED STATES

The Americans have a more extensive experience of job enrichment than any individual European country. But much of the associated literature relates to attitudes towards concepts such as responsibility and achievement rather than to case studies and experiments in the re-design of jobs. In this, it corresponds to some extent with the pattern that

Wilkinson found in Europe. The great bulk of these attitude reviews support Herzberg's two-factor theory and lend credence to the potential for job enrichment. Our concern here is to examine some of the practical applications.

Reif and Schoderbek (1966) used a similar point of departure to Wilkinson. Recognizing that the emphasis was all too often on the reaction of the worker, they turned their attention to the manager's criterion of cost. They sent questionnaires to 276 of the larger companies in the USA and received 210 replies; 169 or 80·5 per cent of these were not using any form of job enlargement.* Amongst those who had introduced job enlargement the main advantages, in descending order of importance, were: increased job satisfaction, reduced costs, better quality, better quantity of work and a decrease in monotony. The major disadvantage, also highlighted by Wilkinson, was that of overcoming resistance to change: following this came 'some workers not capable of growing with the job', 'increased training time' and union opposition. All the companies concerned thought the applications were at least 'successful': their criteria for success were first and foremost profit followed by attitude and morale. The lack of any respondents with unsuccessful applications points to possible biases in the returns.

One of the first organizations to introduce job enrichment in the USA was International Business Machines [IBM] (Walker, 1950; Richardson and Walker, 1948). This policy has continued and Maher *et al* (1970) have reported the improvements which accrued from a fairly typical job enrichment exercise. Instead of inspection at various stages along the production process, a change was introduced whereby inspection was only carried out at the end, whilst some inspectors were moved to a 'machine quality assurance department' with a variety of functions over which

* Job enlargement included the introduction of a greater variety of knowledge and skill, fuller use of cognitive and motor abilities and more freedom and responsibility in task performance.

they had considerable autonomy. The results were a notable improvement in attitudes and morale and also a number of marked changes in performance along 10 separate dimensions; for example:

"improvement in the acceptance rate of purchased production parts from 92·9 to 97·5 per cent".
"a reduction of more than 50 per cent in defective quality lots found in assembly".
"a 50 per cent reduction in the time needed to inspect purchased parts" (Maher, 1970).

Two American organizations which have been closely associated with the application of the behavioural sciences and with job enrichment in particular are Texas Instruments and the American Telephone and Telegraph Company. Both have introduced job enrichment at all levels of the organization. In one extreme example (Weed, 1971), Texas Instruments enriched the jobs of general office cleaners and 'restroom'cleaners. In the offices, contract cleaners, paid $1.40 per hour and with a labour turnover rate of approximately 400 per cent per annum produced a cleaning performance which was 65 per cent perfect. Permanent staff were recruited instead and paid a minimum of $1.80 per hour. There was some re-design of working arrangements with the objective of providing workers with more scope for the planning and control of their jobs, but more attention seems to have been given to inculcating loyalty to Texas Instruments. The result was a performance level of 85 per cent, a reduction in labour turnover to under 40 per cent and a reduction in the numbers required from 120 to 71. Although studies of this type are often claimed as examples of its success, it is hard to isolate the impact of any job enrichment. Furthermore, in this particular example the performance criteria were open to bias.

The work carried out at the American Telephone and Telegraph Company (Ford, 1969) is in some respects more impressive. They have come closest to the kind of experimental study, using control groups, which ICI tried out

167

and in certain cases they appear to have introduced job enrichment without any associated increases in pay. Furthermore, they are exceptional in producing evidence of unsuccessful as well as highly successful applications. As at ICI, shop floor workers were involved in the least successful experiments but they also had some success at this level. For example, with framemen, who had to wire up telecommunications frames, a set of highly fragmented tasks were turned into a more meaningful total job for small work groups. The result was an almost 100 per cent increase in the number of orders completed on time and a notable increase in job satisfaction as measured by the number of grievances. Some of those who were involved in implementing these early experiments subsequently went to other organizations or into consultancy to continue this type of work. For example Janson (1971) has produced impressive results from experiments, using control groups, with auditing clerks and typists. In particular, he was able to demonstrate dramatic improvements in quality.

Once again the emphasis is on improvements in quality. This is not a random finding. Although quality improvements came third on the list of advantages in the Reif and Schoderbek survey, in his review of the subject Lawler (1969) found that, whilst all 10 of the studies he covered reported improvements in quality, only four reported higher productivity. The most penetrating analysis of the American studies is that of Hulin and Blood (1968). They comment that many of the earlier studies, which reported apparent success with job enrichment lacked control groups and objective criteria against which to analyse results.

CONCLUSION

In the preceding section we have reviewed some of the better known studies of job enrichment. In addition to these there are many more examples of situations when a redesign of jobs has led to job enrichment or to the development of autonomous work groups; often these will have been part of a more conventional change rather than a conscious attempt to increase worker motivation. A question-mark hangs over the general validity of the evidence since many organizations are, quite naturally, reluctant to publicize any failures. Furthermore, many of the better known case studies are provided by individuals who are fully committed to the idea of job enrichment or autonomous work groups. We are now in a better position to answer some of the questions posed earlier in the chapter which asked whether or not this approach actually gave the worker greater control, whether or not he used any such control and, if he did, what impact it had.

Turning to the first question, it is clear that generally the worker does obtain greater control. This is usually limited to job-specific issues and is not widely considered to have a significant impact on collective bargaining. On the other hand it would be wrong totally to discount any such influence without more detailed investigation, particularly where collective bargaining forms the framework within which changes in job design are introduced. The extent of the control is limited by constraints imposed primarily by the technology and by the amount of risk the manager is prepared to take. These constraints are examined in more detail in the following chapter. This second consideration has often meant that workers have been given control over how to do their job rather than over its purpose and targets. However, one may almost inevitably lead to the other. Clearly the continued opportunity to exert this control depends upon how it is used but, as Wilkinson (1971) points out, once it is underway this process can be extremely difficult to reverse.

Moving to the second question, the available evidence suggests that workers will use their control only when they feel that their primary concerns for pay, job security and interpersonal relations have been safeguarded or enhanced and when they perceive that they will gain from the situation. Therefore the ICI process operators (Paul, 1969) rejected the opportunity to maintain plant 'efficiencies' but did agree to arrange cover for breaks. The distinction between the primary and secondary concerns of the work-force is aptly demonstrated in Daniel's (1970) study of a productivity deal among petrochemical workers, which also involved elements of job enrichment and to which we referred in chapter 2. The initial agreement met with considerable opposition because, despite no-redundancy guarantees, it was seen as a threat to security. Nine months later, when it was quite apparent that their security was not threatened, the workers reported satisfaction with the new situation and in particular with the aspect which had changed most noticeably – the job content. This supports a general conclusion that many blue-collar workers in the United Kingdom are neither strongly for nor against job enrichment or autonomous work groups. The available evidence indicates that they are more likely to ignore the control it provides than to use this control to oppose management. At the same time it would be wrong to ignore cultural differences and it may be that workers in, for example, Scandinavia give higher priority to their job content.

Finally, in answer to the third question, there is wide agreement that changes in job design are generally associated with increases in both productivity and job satisfaction. But when considering blue-collar workers it would be wrong to attribute such increases to the changes in job content and therefore, presumably, to a consequent increase in worker motivation. This limitation is necessary because the impact of any changes seems to be closely related to the way in which the changes are introduced. Throughout this chapter we have focused upon Herzberg's motivational approach, which emphasizes the benefits of job enrichment to the individual and which implies that changes in job content, since they operate on a separate dimension from other job factors, can be viewed in isolation and therefore introduced into the work environment in isolation. This is the approach which has attracted most attention among managers and it has met with a certain amount of success in

America and among managerial, professional and white-collar workers in the United Kingdom. In the United Kingdom and the rest of Europe it is usually unacceptable to blue-collar workers, many of whom are likely to view it as manipulative. Instead, a socio-technical systems perspective may be more appropriate. This would suggest that the social, technological and economic factors are inter-related and cannot be viewed in isolation; therefore they cannot be significantly changed in isolation. It follows that a successful approach to the introduction of changes in job design is likely to require a detailed analysis of the social system, the technical system, the communication and information system and the payment system. In addition, repercussions on the management hierarchy cannot be ignored. The result of any such analysis is that a number of inter-related factors are likely to be altered more or less simultaneously and it becomes impossible to identify the impact of any one factor in isolation. If it were possible to do so, one could, in theory at least, attribute much of the increase in productivity and satisfaction to an increase in pay and to a more effective organization of work rather than to the impact of any changes in job design on worker motivation. The strategies implied by the use of this socio-technical systems perspective, which often though not always results in autonomous work groups rather than job enrichment, are described in a series of papers edited by Davis and Taylor (1972).

Summary

This chapter has examined the nature and impact of the control provided by changes in job design resulting in job enrichment or autonomous work groups. Both approaches can increase the amount of control each worker can exert over his own job by providing him with more responsibility, autonomy and scope for achievement. Since the possibilities offered by this type of control are currently attracting considerable attention, the more widely known of the underlying theories is examined in some detail.

Herzberg's (1959, 1966) motivator-hygiene theory has

provided a starting point for many managers who have become interested in job design as a basis for increasing worker motivation. Socio-technical systems theory provides an alternative theoretical perspective but, despite its more sensible approach to change, its greater complexity has failed to attract management to the same extent. Motivator-hygiene theory argues that there are two separate dimensions to job satisfaction; one, which is termed the hygiene dimension, is concerned with the need to avoid dissatisfaction and includes factors extrinsic to the job such as security, pay, supervision and company policy. The other dimension, termed the motivator dimension, is concerned with the factors leading to positive satisfaction, high motivation and high performance; these factors are all associated with the job content and include achievement, personal growth and responsibility. A brief review is sufficient to indicate that the theoretical foundations of this approach are weak; it is based on a doubtful methodology, the original findings lend only tenuous support and subsequent research in the United Kingdom on blue-collar workers has failed to support it.

In the reported literature, the impact of job enrichment has generally been positive in that it has led to increased productivity and job satisfaction: but this has only occurred when the workers believed that their pay, security and interpersonal relations had been safeguarded or enchanced. Furthermore the way in which the changes were introduced had an important bearing on their impact; in particular, changes in job content alone were unlikely to be successful. This suggests that the socio-technical systems approach is likely to produce better results than a strategy based on the motivator-hygiene theory. This would take account of the inter-related social, technical, financial and information systems which help to determine the nature of the change and its potential effectiveness. Given that such an approach is adopted and the workers view of the situation is favourable, as long as it remains favourable they will generally use the control offered through the re-design of jobs to further managerial goals.

CHAPTER EIGHT

ORGANIZATIONAL CONSTRAINTS AND PARTICIPATION

In this chapter, we turn our attention to some of the problems associated with direct participation which can be seen as arising from organizational form. The discussion will be sub-divided in the following ways: an analysis of those aspects of organizational structure which constrain the possibilities of task participation; secondly, these constraints will be viewed as risks in the decision-making process; finally, there will be a critical discussion of various perspectives of organizational analysis and their relevance to direct participation.

THE NATURE OF ORGANIZATIONAL CONSTRAINTS

Constraints have been seen by Reeves, Turner and Woodward, for example, as "all those elements or features of an organization which impinge on employees to decide or limit the behavioural content of their work" (Woodward, 1970, p 9). We are widening that perspective to include forms of uncertainty and risk as constraints. This is similar to the motivational framework developed in chapter 3. The predicted outcomes of a particular strategy will be weighed against the desirability of other perceived alternatives, and will take account of the ease of attainment and of the overall degree of predictability. Using a similar argument Thompson and Tuden (1959) have suggested that decisions always involve two major elements:

1 beliefs about cause/effect relationships and
2 preference regarding possible outcomes.

The constraints discussed below have an impact upon the

level of risk and uncertainty in terms of the relationship between the cause, that is the participative programme, and the effects of such a programme. In the present context, it will become apparent that a decision to implement participative schemes can be based upon value systems rather than upon evidence about any clear-cut cause/effect relationship.

As constraints, the following variables are considered to be particularly relevant:

1 Technology and control systems
2 The product market
3 Labour costs
4 Interest groups.

The list is not intended to be exhaustive but merely to draw attention to what are generally accepted to be the major organizational constraints on direct participation. Nor is it suggested that these variables are independent; in our discussion, particular relationships will become apparent.

TECHNOLOGY[1] AS A CONSTRAINT ON PARTICIPATION

In recent years, an extensive amount of research has been undertaken on the nature and implications of certain systems of technology. Two distinct approaches can be detected:
(i) There are those who, following a Marxian tradition, have largely concentrated their resources upon the concept of alienation. The concept, which was discussed briefly in chapter 3, is relevant to participation as it concerns itself *inter alia* with the relationship between the worker and the production system. Alienation is a widely used word and has probably suffered as a result. An acceptable working definition is that suggested by Parker *et al* (1967, p 168), who feel that alienation has been used "to embrace both attributes of roles in terms of their inability to afford meaning, control and social integration to occupants as well as the consequent subjective experience of individuals in terms of non-involvement and self-estrangement". Because

participation is inevitably concerned with control and involvement, the existence of what might be called alienating factors becomes central to a discussion of participation.

(ii) There are those whose main interest lies in organization theory and who, whilst stressing that there is no one best system of organization, acknowledge the importance of technology as a major determinant of organizational structure. Whereas the first approach has developed largely from the study of the individual, this latter approach is more concerned with the organization as a total system.

ALIENATION AND TECHNOLOGICAL CONSTRAINTS

Probably the best known and most representative example of the first approach is contained in Blauner's work (1964). His approach is dependent upon seeing technology as the main cause of alienation; the social relations inherent in capitalism are considered irrelevant in this respect. Given this primary concern with technological systems, Blauner has distinguished four types of manufacturing[2] technology: craft, machine-minding, assembly line and continuous process. As one moves from craft through to continuous process industries, mechanization and product standardization tend to increase. Touraine (in C R Walker (ed), 1962) has recognized a similar evolutionary process, namely the disintegration of the worker's traditional skills and the development of mechanical processes. Although the four typologies envisaged by Blauner can and do co-exist in the same enterprise, their relevance for the present context is that, as discrete systems, they permit differing degrees of control over task performance. In mass production industries, Blauner saw the vast majority of decisions concerning methods and techniques being determined by engineers, foremen and time-study men, and he concluded that "only craftsmen and the few blue-collar operators in the new automated industries have much opportunity to introduce their own ideas in the course of their work" (1964, p 171).

Consistent with this perspective, the automobile industry's assembly-line technology has been described as "the classic symbol of the subjection of man to the machine" (Walker and Guest, 1952, p 9). Whilst we would agree with those who argue that the opportunities for the exercise of discretion by the assembly-line worker are severely circumscribed, it would be wrong to attribute objective alienating characteristics to this form of technology. It would be equally fallacious to view alienation in totally subjective terms, that is by examining definitions of social structure without understanding the importance of social structure upon definitions. Goldthorpe *et al* (1968) seems to have made that mistake in arguing that behaviour and attitudes can be explained by an understanding of the meanings and definitions attached to the work situation. Furthermore it must be remembered that, even though the performance of a particular set of tasks might not be intrinsically satisfying, satisfaction may be derived, for example, from social relations at work or because work provides the means to satisfy certain extra-work goals. Nevertheless, even among the sample of workers, described by Goldthorpe *et al* (1968), who displayed such a high level of instrumentality in their work attitudes, the assemblers showed a noticeable preference for more variation and enlargement in their jobs, and could be seen as feeling more restricted in relation to the tasks they had to perform than any other group in the sample. In this context, technology was important not for producing dissatisfaction but for lowering the expectations of the workers. They would have preferred variety in their jobs but were content to satisfy themselves with a high level of monetary reward.

An illustration of the impact of technological change is to be found in Chadwick-Jones' (1969) study of the change-over from handmills to fully automated processes in the tinplate industry. In the handmills, the everyday decisions relating to the rolling and tinning of steel were generally within the technical competence of the operatives. The autonomy of the team was further reinforced by the union's control over discipline and promotion. Chadwick-Jones provides the following example of the workers' freedom to take decisions:

"The six operatives used judgements in taking decisions on the number of steel bars to be rolled during the work cycle, and this depended partly on their variation in temperature during the rolling operations. Here the operative was guided by the colour of steel and by the Kinaesthetic cues drawn through its 'bounce' on the floor of the mill" (1969, p 14).

Whilst the introduction of the new technology increased output per worker tenfold, at the same time it imposed severe limitations upon the worker's freedom to control his set of tasks. Chadwick-Jones argued that the main characteristic of the change in tinplate technology centred upon the removal of many of the decision requirements from the worker's role. In other words, the benefits of the new technology in terms of costs and productivity were not compatible with the worker's desire to control the performance of his set of tasks.

A significant characteristic of the more automated technologies noted by Chadwick-Jones, and also by Woodward (1965) in her earlier study, was the increased intervention in the production process of technical and maintenance staff. This point is illustrated by the changing composition of the labour force in the steel industry; whereas in 1950 nine per cent of the labour force could be classified as administrative, technical or clerical, by 1968, with a smaller total labour force, 24 per cent fell into this category. In the context of the tinplate industry, Chadwick-Jones noted that technicians became responsible for quality checks and the testing of electrolyte samples, whilst at the same time specialist branches of management developed to control and support these functions.

The dependence on technical expertise in advanced technologies is particularly well illustrated in the hot mill of a modern steel works. The duties of the operatives in the mill largely consist of monitoring dials in a control room located several feet above the rolling processes. Dials are controlled according to instructions and orders received from the quality control and computer personnel; these are the groups responsible for production and quality control. In these circumstances, the operatives' jobs require only a minimal acquaintance with the techniques used by the computer and laboratory staff.

This process of disintegration of the workers' skills is by no means confined to manual workers. In the white collar sector, recent years have witnessed an increasing division of labour, reinforced by the spread of larger administrative units and the intervention of computer techniques (see Mumford and Banks, 1967). The clerk, for example, is now less likely to control a whole clerical process and is more likely to find himself responsible for the preparation of data for processing. It could be argued that an increasing division of labour, larger work units and more limited promotion opportunities are some of the important factors that have influenced the growth of white-collar unionism (Bain, 1970; Roberts, Loveridge and Gennard, 1972).

Using the Blauner typology of technologies, it is generally accepted that craft industries provide greater scope for direct participation. According to Blauner "the freedom to determine techniques of work, to choose one's tools, and to vary the sequence of the operations, is part of the nature and traditions of craftsmanship" (1964, p 43). These freedoms were not as real for other workers. According to the Roper survey, on which Blauner based his conclusions, 49 per cent of factory workers said that they were able to try out their own ideas in contrast to more than three-quarters of the printers (taken as a representative craft group) who reported this work freedom.

In relation to the performance of particular sets of tasks, the nature of technology assumes importance for two reasons; it determines both the opportunities for the exercise of discretion by the worker and the level and content of technical expertise. Dealing with the latter point, Chadwick-Jones (1969) has argued that, as the degree of automation increases, a falling curve might be demonstrated for direct intervention in the production process by semi-skilled workers. If this is the case, it has a special relevance in the present context; if the intention is to facilitate direct participation, it would appear necessary, particularly in the case of the more automated technologies, to acquaint the participant with some of the technical knowledge essential for the production process. To many managers, such a move could be construed as imposing a less rigorous control over the production process. Nevertheless the case study described by Cotgrove, Dunham and Vamplew (1971), discussed in greater detail in the previous chapter, referred to an automated technology in which, under a productivity agreement, workers had been given a responsibility for manning and scheduling, previously determined by computer processes. The changeover appeared to be successful.[3]

ORGANIZATION THEORY AND TECHNOLOGICAL CONSTRAINTS

The other body of research has emphasized the importance of the technology variable as a key determinant of organization structure. Woodward (1965), in her South East Essex study, classified firms according to their overall technological complexity into (i) unit and small batch production; (ii) large batch and mass production and (iii) process production. She found that certain structural characteristics, such as the ratio of supervision and management to the total personnel and the nature of decision making, could be related to the technology. But there were more similarities between organizations with batch and process systems than there were between these and those with mass production systems. The methods of control established for the production process provided a theme for Woodward's later work (1970), and she seemed to modify her original hypothesis to suggest that organizational structure is not so much a function of technology as of control systems. Following Eilon (1962), a management control system can be seen as containing the four elements of objective setting, planning, executive execution and control, although they should not be regarded as discrete or sequential elements in the management process. In other words, control systems provide a means of directing and administering the production process. In the present context, the nature of control systems becomes relevant in that they can be seen as impinging upon the methods of task performance.

Reeves and Woodward (1970) have distinguished between control systems on two dimensions which are concerned with the degree of impersonality of control and the complexity of the control. Looking at the first of these, they have suggested it might be possible to place a firm on a scale ranging from personal hierarchical[4] control at one extreme to completely mechanical control at the other. Between these two extremes come the administrative, but impersonal, control processes. Given a movement towards more mechanical systems of control, the key functions of management will concentrate increasingly upon the establishment of planning criteria on which control objectives can be based. The nature of the process gains relevance in the present context in so far as it can affect the role of the production worker. "Where the control processes are personal, the operators are more likely to be producers in the exact sense of the word; collectively, they make the products that go out of the factory gate. When the control processes become mechanical, however, the operators increasingly cease to be responsible for making the product. They may monitor its manufacture or their role may be that of controllers of control. Where control is administrative, but impersonal, there are elements of both roles in the production operator's task" (1970, p 46).

From these statements it is possible to suggest that certain modifications in existing control systems would have to be made in order to accommodate participative ideas designed to extend the decision-making requirements of the worker's task. For example, the personal and administrative systems would have to allow a greater sharing of power in those decisions concerned with the utilization of labour resources. The essential nature of the mechanical system would have to be modified to allow workers to be involved in the planning process and this could only occur effectively after an introduction to the necessary techniques. There would be a greater need to understand the system as a whole, instead of just those aspects that relate to the immediate task environment. This reinforces the point made earlier that the introduction of direct participation in certain systems of work depends to a great extent upon the workers' task being widened to include technical and planning decisions.

The relevance of risk becomes apparent at this point. Systems of control often achieve an air of permanency and rationality that makes changes appear particularly hazardous. In addition, there would be a need to reverse a deliberate management policy towards specialization in planning, technical and research matters (Thomason, 1970). Whilst the nature of the control system will be mainly dependent upon the technology and product market of the enterprise, Ingham found, in his study of the size effect upon organizational[5] structure and behaviour, that "within the limits imposed by technology the workers in the small[6] firm possessed a great deal of autonomy in the production process" (1970, p 77). This meant that job rotation was higher in the smaller firms than in either of the larger plants in Ingham's sample. In one of the larger plants which had a high degree of bureaucratization and a mass production technology, there was a very low level of job rotation. There is little evidence to suggest that size necessarily determines the type of technology but it does seem to be related to certain bureaucratic indices such as impersonal controls and specialization. (Pugh et al, 1969; Ingham, 1970; Hinings and Lee, 1971). In other words, impersonal control systems are more likely to be found in larger organizations. A possible indication of this is that a series of studies (Indik, 1963; Ingham, 1970) has found greater levels of satisfaction in small plants. For instance, strikes, absenteeism and labour turnover increased with the size of organizations.

Turning to their second dimension, Reeves and Woodward (1970) differentiate control systems according to whether they are single system (unitary) or multi-system (fragmentary). It was found, for instance, that in some firms efforts were made to relate the standards set for different departments and functions into an integrated system of control. On the other hand, there were those firms which did not attempt to relate departments and standards, maybe as a result of producing a number of different products or because of the emphasis upon quality in some processes. In such circumstances, multi-system control emerged and could be seen as creating a state of uncertainty, as different and not always compatible goals were pursued simultaneously. For example, the aim of a supervisor in such a system would be to violate each of the standards as little as possible. Such uncertainty and conflict would not exist within a unitary system.

The two dimensional classification of control systems as envisaged by Reeves and Woodward, produces four distinct categories:

A1 Firms with unitary and mainly personal control
A2 Firms with unitary and mainly impersonal control
B1 Firms with fragmented and mainly personal control
B2 Firms with fragmented and mainly impersonal control.

Figure 4

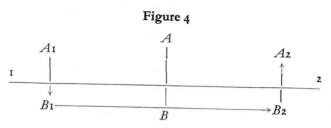

The four distinct categories are set out in Figure 4 and, according to the authors, the normal processes of industrial and technical evolution move a firm in the direction indicated by the arrows. To a certain extent, such a view would seem to give too great a power to evolutionary forces and too little to the wishes and desires of the actors within the system. For example, certain European car manufacturers have re-designed their technologies to allow greater task involvement; increasing labour turnover and an inability to attract labour appear to have been instrumental in persuading management of the desirability of such changes. Nevertheless, those changes are consistent with a concept of risk which emphasizes that managements have the ability to introduce participative schemes; in making such decisions, the perceived gains of participation in relation to systems needs will have to outweigh the costs of changing existing, and apparently rational, control systems.

PRODUCT MARKET

The stability and nature of product markets would appear to be related to control systems; generally the more stable the product environment, the more formally organized the control system. A less stable product market would create a more fluid and dynamic situation. For instance, a firm in the clothing industry is likely to spend a good deal of time upon stimulating demand for new styles, and frequent production changes will be needed to facilitate the introduction of new products. This should result in a more dynamic system of control. A car manufacturer or a chemical firm are less likely to be as preoccupied in this way and can be expected to spend more time on administrative procedures.

Burns and Stalker (1961) have constructed two ideal types of management system. The mechanical model follows similar lines to Weber's classical formulation of bureaucracy, depending upon work role differentiation and hierarchical communication and control. On the other hand, in the organic model, roles are subject to constant changes and a variety of sources of control and communication. In this case, the emphasis within the organization is upon reviewing ends, rather than the administration of stable means. The authors were not suggesting that one model was intrinsically superior to the other, only that each model was more appropriate for a particular environment. For an organization faced with fairly rapid changes in technologies and product, the organic model had advantages, since it can make it possible to base authority more upon expertise than upon hierarchical position. On the other hand, those firms with a stable product market might find it more appropriate to approximate to the mechanical model. As for the nature of tasks, March and Simon (1958, p 159) have commented, in a similar way, that "process specialization will be carried furthest in stable environments and that under rapidly changing circumstances specialization will be sacrificed to secure greater self-containment of separate programmes". Both March and Simon (1958) and Burns and Stalker (1961) are suggesting that the division of labour and specialization will be more advanced in those firms with fairly predictable product markets. Nevertheless, it must be remembered that some of the better known experiments with direct participation have taken place in relatively stable environments, such as the chemical and petro-chemical industry. To a great extent, this phenomenon can be explained by reference to the dominance of a managerial ideology which places some emphasis upon participation; an indication that control systems are man-created.

LABOUR COSTS

The impact of schemes of direct participation on labour costs is unclear. The evidence reported in the previous chapters does n ot enable any definitive judgement to be made as to the benefits of job enrichment or autonomous work groups. If we accept that any management introducing participative schemes would hope to extend their control over labour costs and resources, it is not clear whether those firms whose labour costs represent a larger percentage of unit costs are more likely to accept risk than those for whom labour costs constitute a relatively small part of unit costs. In the high cost situation, potential benefits would seem greater as would the risks of failure. Nevertheless, some indications are available to enable us to suggest that the firms with smaller percentage labour costs are more likely to innovate in personnel practices. It will be recalled that the breakthrough in productivity bargaining occurred in the process industries, such as petro-chemicals. It took time for the experiences in these industries to be universally accepted as beneficial, possibly because it was realized that the commercial implications of failure were more immediate in unit and mass production firms. A possible conclusion to be drawn from this is that, in some cases, technology increases risk whilst at the same time encouraging a tight administration of labour practices. It is also worth noting that one of the more important experiments with direct participation has occureed in ICI, a firm with a largely continuous process technology, in which labour costs represent a smaller proportion of unit costs.

THE ROLE OF INTEREST GROUPS

Any industrial organization will contain various interest groups, whose ends will not always appear to be overtly compatible. Trade unions normally represent the most significant of such groups, and it is possible that they might see in direct participation, particularly when it involves redesigning jobs, a threat to their traditional interest in work practices and wage differentials. The craft system, for instance, has encouraged exclusiveness and a reluctance to accept that non-craft workers are capable of performing tasks which historically are the responsibility of skilled men. The type of job enrichment proposed by Chadwick-Jones (1969), involving production workers in simple maintenance tasks, has been rejected by craft workers in many productivity negotiations. A similar rejection has been found among technical workers faced with 'work structuring' proposals (see Roberts, Loveridge and Gennard (1972)).

Direct participation through job enrichment might activate the conflict contained in the skilled/unskilled distinction; it might also challenge existing and traditional wage differentials, particularly if additional payments were made for the acceptance of more responsible or demanding work. These are the very problems that have been found in productivity negotiations, and the often similar form of job enrichment proposals may encourage a similar trade union reaction.

In addition, an analysis of the discussion of participation and industrial democracy within the labour movement would seem to indicate a near total concern with indirect, as opposed to direct, forms of participation. The interest has mainly centred on consultation and board representation in the nationalized industries, and the structure of collective bargaining in industry generally. The functions of trade unions have been defined as achieving fair wages, good conditions and job security for their members; job interest has ranked as a low priority. In the 1920s Goodrich (1920) made a similar point, noting that unions had been preoccupied with maintaining the jobs of their members; they had therefore paid little attention to the type of work their people did. Although there have been many social and economic changes since Goodrich's time, there appears to have been a remarkable consistency in trade union priorities. For many trade unionists, proposals to restructure work tasks will be received as the basis for negotiation in the same way as productivity proposals. This is not necessarily a bad thing; the previous discussion of job design has suggested that the methods of introducing change are related to the possible success of such changes.

The shareholders of privately-owned enterprises represent another interest group or, in Rhenman's (1969) terminology, another stakeholder. Shareholders are primarily interested in profitability and return on capital. The pressure of their interest is likely to be towards a good return on capital. They could therefore constitute an effective constraint upon a management, particularly if the financial implications of participation are uncertain. Equally, groups of middle and junior managers have an interest in forms of participation. Increasing the status and responsibility of the worker could be construed by managers as a deliberate attempt to lessen their own influence and authority; for this reason they might attempt to reject or at least contain schemes of worker participation. Evidence of such behaviour can be found in the reaction of managers to the appointment of employee directors in the BSC (Brannen *et al*, 1972).

This brief discussion of interest groups has been introduced to draw attention to some of the complexities of change. Various groups related to the organization will approach participation with differing definitions and goals and their varied reactions will have to be accommodated.

DECISION-MAKING, CONSTRAINTS AND RISK

Throughout the preceding discussion of organizational constraints we have emphasized, by implication, the element of risk in decision-making. This notion is important in two respects. It shows that management takes decisions on a basis that is not dissimilar to the strategies outlined in the expectancy model: they will weigh up the rewards and the costs involved and evaluate these in terms of the predictability of the various outcomes – in other words, in terms of the risk. It also shows that the organization of work is, in part at least, socially determined. Both these points underline Hyman's comment (1972, p 101) that "whether the consequences of technology are in fact liberating or enslaving depends on *how* it is decided to use the machines, and *who* makes the decision. To attribute unpleasant social consequences to inanimate machinery is to evade examining the *human* actions which – deliberately or by default – are in fact responsible."

In theory, the proposals for direct participation which

form the substance of this book aim to offer more liberating and demanding work for the individual. The implementation of such schemes gives rise to risk because it places control over aspects of production and management in the hands of the workers. A number of studies of managers (see Nichols, 1969; Sofer, 1970) and the data on management attitudes presented in chapter 4 indicate that managers continue to place a particularly high value on profit and efficiency and use these among their main criteria of success. If so, it follows that participation will be considered in instrumental terms – that is, by measuring the contribution that participation can make towards organizational objectives. A concern for the content of work and for human nature will necessarily be subordinated to other more quantifiable objectives. On the other hand, the advocates of direct participation would argue that the risks may outweigh the costs of maintaining an existing production system which takes no account of intrinsic job satisfaction and can lead to high levels of boredom, frustration and various forms of aggression such as absenteeism and frequent disputes. But in this context, it is relevant to note that the evidence introduced in previous chapters has indicated no clear-cut relationship between the introduction of direct participation *per se* and increased efficiency. The manager will look for such a relationship and, in its absence, might prefer the familiar predictability of existing technological and control systems.

Our discussion of certain organizational variables has served to illustrate their relationship to direct participation, and the extent to which participative schemes involve an element of risk. Too often the advocates of participation have minimized or ignored the impact of certain organizational variables.

PERSPECTIVES IN ORGANIZATIONAL ANALYSIS

The value of any analysis of organizational constraints depends partly upon the relevance of the perspective adopted. Therefore in this section we look briefly at the strengths and weaknesses of a purely technological perspective, of socio-technical systems theory and of the action frame of reference. Attempts to explain behaviour in formal organizations have generally taken a particular feature of the organization as their starting point. In the case of human relations, the emphasis was upon the role of the work group, and particularly upon the need for socially skilled superiors. The significance of this school of thought, along with later developments in neo-human relations, has been fully discussed in previous chapters. Other writers have stressed the importance of technology for behaviour and, in some cases, to such an extent that technology has been seen as almost the sole determinant of behaviour. For instance, Sayles (1969, pp 4–5) concluded that his study indicated "that the technology of the plant moulds the type of work group that evolves. . . . The human element, so-called, is a resultant of the technological decisions, and in part at least, predictable from them". Using this perspective in his own research, Sayles distinguished between four types of work group, according to their level of skill and their interpersonal interaction. Apathetic groups had limited grievance activity and no clearly defined leadership, in contrast to the erratic groups whose leadership was highly centralized and for whom the level of grievance activity was high, although often poorly controlled. Strategic groups pursued their grievances in a rational and continuous manner; in so doing, they developed an internal coherence and generally were active participants in the affairs of the union. The final group, the conservatives, were less involved in trade unionism although they would use pressure to redress their grievances. Despite changes in the composition of the groups, their behaviour remained remarkably consistent and Sayles explained this phenomenon by reference to the social structure and the system of production of the organization. At the time, Sayles's work represented a break from the traditional human relations approach by acknowledging the different perceived needs of interest groups. But it can be

189

criticized for its failure to take into account extra-work variables that influence behaviour, and for not paying enough attention to the power of trade unions.

An alternative and more sophisticated perspective is to be found in the writing of those who, perceiving organizations in terms of socio-technical systems, have argued strongly for the restructuring of tasks. Generally adopting a psychological approach, the socio-technical system theorists have stressed the inter-relationship between technology, environment, the sentiment of members and organizational form. In order to achieve increased efficiency, it is seen as necessary to optimize all these elements. According to Silverman (1970) the objective of this approach is to design formal structures that can most effectively relate to one another the varied demands of environment, technology and members.

In relation to the individual, the emphasis has necessarily been placed upon the nature of tasks with a view to optimizing intrinsic job satisfaction. For instance, Emery (1966, p 6) has concluded that "the requirements of an individual in an industrial setting are such that the most potent form of engaging the worker's interest and the only alternative to the reward and punishment procedure is to move towards a design that can cope with the tasks arising from the technology and in addition to design their jobs in such a way as to create conditions for what we will call task involvement".

A great deal of the research conducted with this socio-technical perspective has been largely prescriptive and, as such, has not always been based upon a coherent research framework. Nevertheless, some interesting findings have emerged. Probably the best known study is that by Trist and Bamforth (1951), which deals with the process of mechanization of coal mines in NW Durham. The traditional system of coal getting had been carried out by largely autonomous work groups in which each individual generally possessed several skills. The introduction of long-wall mining necessitated a 'factory' type system, with increasing mechanization and a greater division of labour. The expected improvements in productivity did not materialize. Consequently, the research team concentrated its activities on creating a new approach which would harmonize social needs and technical demands. The new system allowed for job rotation, thereby giving the worker wider responsibility and at the same time making use of the miners' multiple skills in the context of a working group. A change in the role of supervision and management meant that supporting services were provided rather than direct supervision. The apparent success of the changeover confirmed the researchers' belief in the desirability of the socio-technical perspective.

From a consultancy or prescriptive viewpoint, it would be difficult to deny the usefulness of this approach. In the present context two criticisms should be made: first, there seems to be a generalized implicit assumption about motivation, stressing the importance of intrinsic task satisfaction, combined with a reluctance to accept the part that extra-work variables might play in shaping orientations to work.

Silverman (1970), for instance, criticizes the assumption made by Trist *et al* (1963) that "the type of attachment to work of the Durham miner is repeated among other workers and that all would be satisfied in the same work-setting" (1970, p 123).

Secondly, it can be argued that the socio-technical perspective fails to distinguish rigorously between those factors which determine the structure of an organization, and those that can be used to measure the effectiveness of the existing set-up. For example, the existence of a 'healthy' work group can be seen as both a determinant of organization shape, as well as an indicator of effectiveness. If so, no general guide-lines can be provided to indicate the degree of freedom to change certain variables, or indeed the risk attached to such changes. The nature of such variables might preclude radical organizational change.

Despite the noteworthy practical success of the

socio-technical perspective, it has failed to attract much support amongst managers. The lack of popularity might be explained by a preference for the perceived predictability and simplicity of alternatives compared with the complexity of the socio-technical system concept, and the difficulties of measuring socio-technical systems. Another possible explanation may be the existence of a fairly widespread belief among managers that, in the efficient factory, technical systems alone determine the level of productivity; by implication, they would see no need for non-technical workers to understand such systems, nor for the worker to be consulted about productivity. Such changes might be interpreted as involving an unnecessary risk when compared with the predictability of technical systems.

In recent years, there has been a significant movement away from empirical studies relating aspects of organizational structure to behaviour, and an increasing tendency to adopt an action frame of reference (Silverman, 1970) to analyse the differing orientations that people bring to their work. It thus becomes possible to explain variations in behaviour despite the technical and even social similarities of an organization. Goldthorpe (1964, quoted in Ingham, 1970, p 47) has suggested that a social action approach to industrial behaviour is dependent upon the following explicit propositions:

1 Workers tend to form partly self-selected relatively homogeneous workforces.
2 Particularly under conditions of full employment, this homogeneity is partly the result of choices made by workers to meet their needs and aspirations.
3 Because of this homogeneity, groups of workers in a particular organization can be expected to have common attitudes towards work which will help to determine their behaviour.
4 These common attitudes about the work situation will, to some extent, reside in factors outside the work environment.

Whilst we might hold some reservations about these assumptions, particularly in so far as it appears that the individual is capable of a completely rational choice, the value of the social action approach lies in the emphasis given to extra-work variables. Position in the class structure, social aspirations and the importance of traditional communities are just examples of the many variables that it would be permissible to use to explain industrial behaviour.

In their study of industrial behaviour, Goldthorpe *et al* (1968) distinguished between three basic orientations to work: instrumental, solidaristic and bureaucratic. They found that their sample of workers attached a largely instrumental meaning to work; consequently intrinsic job satisfaction was regarded as of little importance since work was essentially defined as the provision of means to achieve certain extra-work ends. Such findings indicate that the workers have adjusted to their work as it is, and are largely unconcerned with work as it should be. The meanings they attach to work are not significantly influenced by the structure of the work situation.

An action frame of reference in relation to orientations to work is valuable because it avoids prescriptive assumptions about motivation, and about those aspects of work that are considered by others to be important to the worker. However, there are potential dangers in the action perspective; it would often appear that the actor's definitions are seen as sufficient explanations of behaviour. This ignores the interaction between social structure and meaning. As Friedricks (1972, p 269) has argued, "man not only creates his everyday world (the process of objectivation), but it turns round to produce him in turn". There is a need for a dialectical sociology, based upon the interaction of social structure and social consciousness. This would suggest, in the present discussion of organizations, behaviour and participation, a need to analyse the complex interaction between organizational structure and definitions of that structure. In other words, when dealing with technology, it is essential to recognize that it largely determines the objective possibilities for direct participation, whilst at the same time influencing the meanings given to participation. This approach would consider that neither structure nor meaning alone constitute adequate explanatory variables; it is the means by which structure shapes meaning, and meaning defines structure that would provide the basis of analysis. In practice this requires an approach which can utilize the strength in the socio-technical approach, the action frame of reference.

Summary

The scope for direct participation will be limited by certain organizational factors, the most important of which is probably the nature of the technology. One approach has focused on the concept of alienation, which is concerned with an individual's inability to control or relate to his environment. Blauner (1964), for example, has argued that alienation increases as one moves from craft through machine minding and assembly line to continuous process technology. Chadwick-Jones (1969) has illustrated this in his description of a change to full automation at a steel plant and the subsequent loss of control suffered by many of the workers. Management reluctance to cede control to the workforce can be explained in terms of the potential risks of such action. Where the possible costs outweigh the expected rewards, management is seldom likely to endorse direct participation.

Woodward (1970) and her colleagues have taken a somewhat different view of technology and have analysed the impact of technological complexity on organization structure and decision-making. In particular, they have presented a model for the analysis of control systems which highlights some of the problems and risks associated with attempts to introduce direct participation.

The product market appears to be another variable which can influence control systems. Generally, the more stable the product market, the more formally organized the control system and the less scope there is for direct participation. Those organizations with lower labour costs as a per cent of unit costs have in the past been more willing to introduce direct participation. Finally, interest groups, and more particularly trade unions, middle managers and shareholders could have a constraining influence. Although technology, product market, labour costs and interest groups represent some of the most significant constraints, the nature and extent of their influence is far from clear.

The particular emphasis adopted in the analysis of organizational constraints has depended to a considerable extent upon the perspective adopted. Sayles (1958), for example, has gone to one extreme by adopting what amounts to technological determinism. The socio-technical systems perspective is far more complex and stresses the need to take account of the interrelationship between social and technical, as well as administrative and attitudinal variables. As a prescriptive model this has had some success (Trist and Bamforth, 1951) but many managers are likely to be put off by its complexity; also, it can be criticized for its implicit assumptions about human motivation. In contrast, the use of an action frame of reference (Goldthorpe et al, 1968) avoids such assumptions by emphasizing the influence of factors outside the work context. But this in turn runs the risk of underestimating the role of organizational structure. The need is therefore for an approach which takes sufficient account of the strengths of both the socio-technical systems perspective and an action frame of reference.

NOTES

1 In their research, Reeves *et al* (Woodward (ed), 1970, p 4) adopted the following working definition of technology: "The collection of plant, machine tools and recipes available at a given time for the execution of the production task and the rationale underlying their utilization".

2 Blauner's typology is concerned solely with the manufacturing sector. Inevitably, with the growth of the non-manufacturing sector, students of organizations are going to be more concerned with classifying technologies in this sector. One such attempt is contained in the work of Thompson (1967) who distinguishes between three types of technology: (a) long-linked technologies (an assembly line), (b) mediatory technologies (insurance firms, banks) and (c) intensive technology (hospitals).

3 The same authors have argued that "the relations between man and machines are substantially determined by the machines themselves" (1971, p 64). This would suggest that in this sort of context they would see only limited opportunities for job enrichment.

4 A system based upon one man's personal authority and influence; subordinates will be structured in a hierarchy, but will work under instructions from that one man.

5 Organization is used here to deal with one location.

6 Under 100.

CHAPTER NINE

INDIVIDUAL CONSTRAINTS AND PARTICIPATION

In his analytic framework for the study of worker participation, Walker (1970) distinguished between participation
potential and the propensity to participate. The participation potential is largely determined by the organizational
constraints which were outlined in the previous chapter.
This chapter examines the individual factors which may
constrain or facilitate the likelihood of participation or the
propensity to participate. These factors can be defined as
those which exist within an individual and which he would
bring to work, irrespective of the type of work he may be
doing. They include such items as his age, ability, previous
experience and personality.

Much of the relevant information in this field is derived
from attitude surveys, therefore a useful starting point is to
examine the differences in outlook which emerge from
broad surveys of attitudes towards participation. From
there, a number of themes can be developed more fully by
reference to other sources of information.

ATTITUDES TOWARDS PARTICIPATION

Although the subject of worker participation has been
extensively discussed and researched, the bulk of the field
work has been designed to evaluate specific participative
programmes rather than to obtain attitudes towards the
concept of participation and towards particular types of
participation (see, for example, Fürstenberg (1969) on co-
determination in Germany, Kolaja (1965) on the Yugoslav
system, and the National Institute of Industrial Psychology
(1952) on joint consultation in the United Kingdom). Many

of the studies are largely descriptive (see, for example, Emery and Thorsrud (1969) and Flanders, Pomeranz and Woodward (1968)); almost all of them are concerned with indirect forms of participation. Even the more comprehensive surveys of attitudes towards participation focus primarily on indirect participation.

One of the earlier surveys of attitudes towards participation was conducted by Holter (1965). This involved 1,128 employees from 17 companies near Oslo and was part of a larger study of sex roles in industry. The results reflected a wide interest in more participation. For the majority, this interest was directed towards decisions relating to their own job. Only a small proportion wanted to participate personally in decisions relating to the company as a whole. This group, which constituted about 14 per cent of the total sample, was described as "an especially well qualified and responsible group of personnel". Those who were interested in more extensive participation were described as "a more active and interested group of personnel" (Holter, 1965) than those who showed no interest in any sort of participation. The study also demonstrated a widespread acceptance of the ability to take on more difficult and demanding work. Unfortunately, beyond the subjective assessments of the type quoted above, little attention was given to individual differences.

Some indication of attitudes towards participation can be gleaned from reports on the Yugoslav system. For example, Kolaja (1965) indicated that there was a high level of apathy among those workers on the management bodies towards the administration and management of the enterprise. Interest was more likely to be aroused when issues of remuneration and welfare were being discussed. Kolaja's study had been criticized because he conducted it in concerns which employed a disproportionately large number of women (see Blumberg, 1968, p 227) and it seems to be generally accepted that women are more apathetic towards the day to day working of a participative system. Nevertheless in Yugoslavia, as elsewhere, it appears that the skilled worker

198

is likely to play a dominating role in the participative system. Blumberg (1968) reports that they comprised less than half the workforce but three-quarters of the members of workers' councils. Another type of individual difference which was particularly noticeable in Yugoslavia was the distinction between the city reared worker and the peasant, who had come to the factory from the land and who had often received virtually no education. Kolaja (1965) noted that these unskilled or semi-skilled workers had a short-term orientation and a concern with immediate gratification. Therefore, in contrast to the more skilled and urbanized workers, they wanted any profits to be distributed among the workforce in preference to re-investing them in the organization.

In a survey which covered 861 employees from 16 Histadruth enterprises in Israel, Tabb and Goldfarb (1970), took into account the likely existence of individual differences in attitude towards participation. Once again the primary focus was upon indirect forms of participation, but direct forms were also included; 57 per cent of the sample accepted as a definition of worker participation that "workers' representatives sit as real members of management, but continue to work at their regular work" (Tabb and Goldfarb, 1970, p 144)[1]. Although manual workers were less inclined to accept this definition than other groups, differences of the magnitude expected by the researchers did not emerge. A number of additional variables was used to search for causes of individual differences; these were age, country of origin, years of residence in the country, plant seniority and schooling. Only length of schooling produced a significant difference; those with less schooling were more likely to see participation only in terms of profit sharing and were more likely to be in favour of a general assembly of workers as the decision-making body[2]. This orientation to profits, in contrast to an acceptance that losses should also be shared, supports the Yugoslav finding that those with less education are more likely to support immediate gratification and see participation in terms of personal rewards.

This less educated group was also less favourably disposed towards other concepts of participation.

This survey demonstrated the importance of previous experience in determining attitudes towards participation. "The enterprises with the lowest percentage of supporters of participation were those that had had the most unsatisfactory experience with it. By contrast, the highest percentage of support came either from enterprises that had had no experience with it or from ones where there was relatively little opposition to it on the part of management" (Tabb and Goldfarb, 1970, p 161).

The brief section on direct forms of participation reveals that 15 per cent felt that, with participation, they would receive more responsible jobs; 21 per cent felt that their supervisors would have to be more considerate and 12 per cent felt that both benefits were likely to occur. These attitudes varied significantly from one occupational group to another: 53 per cent of office workers, 51 per cent of daily-paid manual workers, 43 per cent of foremen and 21 per cent of engineers and technicians visualized positive changes. Those with less than 12 years schooling were significantly more likely to believe that participation would mean more responsibility and/or considerate supervision. Those with less than eight years' schooling were least in favour of participation. In summary, the only factors which consistently demonstrated individual differences in attitude were, as might be expected, occupational group and length of schooling. It is possible that these variables were closely related.

In the United Kingdom, the lack of empirical evidence has stimulated a certain amount of research into attitudes towards worker participation. This has led to some extensive in-company exercises[3]. The United Kingdom has also been involved in the International Labour Office survey (see Clarke, Fatchett, Roberts, 1972) of which the Tabb and Goldfarb work was a part. Two other research programmes are relevant to the present discussion. For a number of years the Medical Research Council Social and Applied

Psychology Unit at Sheffield University has been conducting a series of investigations of attitudes towards participation. One of the specific objectives was to identify and account for individual differences in attitudes towards participation. It makes two observations on the basis of its early results. "One finding which is common to all the organizations studied, is that the more an employee influences the decision-making structure or alternatively perceives that he influences the decision-making structure of the company, then the more he wishes to participate in the company's affairs" (Hespe and Little, 1971, p 343). The second finding is that "the under 26 years age group often express a lower desire for increased participation than their older colleagues" (1971, p 343).

A major study of attitudes towards participation was sponsored by the Government and conducted among just over 2,000 employees of British Rail. In their report, the Tavistock Institute Researchers (Hilgendorf and Irving, 1971) suggest that 88 per cent of the sample would like to see some form of increased participation. The most frequently cited areas for extending participation were through closer contacts between workers and the Board (79 per cent) and improved consultation (44 per cent). By contrast only 14 per cent reported a desire for increased decision-making on the job. The individual differences which emerged largely confirm those already highlighted by other studies. In particular, level of skill and intelligence appear to be important factors. The train men, who are regarded as the skilled group within the industry, already felt they participated in various ways and were interested in extending the amount of participation. In contrast, the mainly unskilled workers at stations and in yards, felt they were less involved in participation at present and were less concerned about having more participation in the future. These findings are consistent with those of Hespe and Little. Age and length of service were strongly inter-related and constituted major influences in apparent contradiction to other findings. Those with longer service tended to feel they already had decision-making power on the job and did not want more; those with less experience (and younger) tended to feel they did not take decisions and wanted to do so in the future. These differences can be accounted for partly, but not totally, by the system of promotion on the basis of seniority. Short-term employees generally had few opinions about participation but, in contrast to older employees, they did have aspirations towards promotion and towards election to representative office.

The investigation obtained a rating of verbal ability which, although not a substitute for a measure of intelligence, was with reservations used as such. The researchers concluded that "while those who are not so fluent are more satisfied and optimistic, verbal ability and perhaps intelligence have no particular effect on attitude to participation. While more verbally able individuals are more critical and active in the organization, the less verbally able are happy but passive, tending to avoid or repudiate those things which would overcomplicate their environment or overstretch their capabilities" (Hilgendorf and Irving, 1971, pp 8–9).

Tests for differences among people from large, medium or small locations demonstrated no clearcut differences. Whether or not size of location is related to urban or rural dimensions was not made clear.

In summary, these surveys of attitudes towards participation do highlight certain individual differences. Interest in participation was related to level of skill among blue-collar employees; those who felt that they already participated to some extent tended to display greater interest in more extensive participation. At the opposite extreme, there was evidence which suggested that there was a fairly large pool of apathetic employees who were not interested in participation except, perhaps, in so far as it provided them with some immediate financial rewards. The evidence on age and education is unclear; however, the common suggestion that it is young workers who want to participate was not strongly supported.

TYPES OF INDIVIDUAL CONSTRAINT

Individual factors, which may constrain or facilitate participation can be divided into three main categories. First,
those which are a function primarily of capacity: these
include intelligence, skill and aptitude. It is probably also
valid to include schooling or education level in this section.
Secondly, there are items which are a function of an individual's inclination or disposition. These would include his
personality, using this concept in its broadest sense and
including variations in susceptibility to group pressures,
previous experience and personal background. Finally, there
might be a third category of situational variables which have
an impact upon individuals or groups. Inside the organization, job level would be one of these; outside the organization financial influences, based on the economy as well as
the requirements of a family must be considered.[4]

1 *Constraints determined by capacity*

It could be argued that those who are less intelligent are less
capable of participating in management decisions. This does
not mean that they are incapable of participating in any way
at the level of their own job, nor does it mean that they are
necessarily uninterested in participation. The majority of
studies has indicated that those who are less intelligent are
generally apathetic towards the idea of participation. In
most of these cases intelligence, perhaps unjustifiably, has
been equated with ability at a particular type of job or with
level of skill. Nevertheless there is a limited number of
studies in which a more careful attempt was made to
measure intelligence. The majority of these have sought to
investigate tolerance of boredom and monotony rather than
participation. Vroom (1964, pp 135–136) has summarized
some of the relevant research and almost all of it confirms
that intelligent workers express more dissatisfaction with
repetitive tasks than less intelligent workers. Purely to
avoid boredom, therefore, they are more likely to welcome

the kind of work situation which allows them some variety and control.

In most studies, only a minority of the workforce expressed a continued and active interest in indirect participation. Sometimes but by no means always the same workers expressed an interest in promotion (see, for example, Banks, 1963). For some of these individuals, a representative role provides them with more challenge and interest than they can find in their day to day work (see Beynon, 1973). Participation in the trade union and shop steward system can provide an outlet for, among others, the more intelligent which may not otherwise be available.

In summarizing the Yugoslav experience of worker participation, Blumberg (1968) has pointed out that "workers' representatives can apparently understand the operation of the enterprise and make sensible, responsible and restrained business decisions, thus offering some refutation to the generally accepted notion that workers are simply incapable of running a factory intelligently" (1968, p 232). Much the same point has been made by writers who have reported on some of the more successful human relations and job enrichment programmes. It may also be significant that there have been virtually no studies which have indicated that inability on the part of the workforce has been a constraint in participative situations: failures have almost always been attributed to negative attitudes. The exceptions are a study by Pym (1965) discussed later in this chapter and the survey of American experience conducted by Reif and Schoderbek (1966), which found that the second most important disadvantage of job enrichment was that some workers were not capable of growing with the job.

The surveys of attitudes towards direct participation, described earlier in this chapter, have presented somewhat contradictory evidence. Hilgendorf and Irving (1971) appear to have indicated that there was an identifiable group of apathetic workers in the lower level jobs. These workers seem to have been both less intelligent as measured by verbal ability and less interested in participation, although the two variables were not directly related. On the other hand, Holter (1965), reported that "the most qualified are as interested in more personal participation in decisions about their own workplace as are the less qualified" (1965, p 303). Talking more broadly, she suggested that those who were uninterested in participation were "relatively often young, women, less qualified employees, who have been a relatively short time in the firm" (1965, p 309). Holter's comments have been partly supported by reviews of the work-structuring programmes conducted at Philips (1968), where it was found that young women were least likely to respond positively though Wild (1973) found that younger women placed a higher value than older women on freedom from control. Smith (1955) partially contradicted some of the studies of the relation between intelligence and monotony by finding that educational level and perception of mon-otony were not related among women.

In summary, the available evidence suggests that level of skill, and probably intelligence, do have some influence on attitudes towards participation. In particular, the more highly skilled are more likely to be interested in both direct and indirect participation and are more prepared to act in a representative capacity. Blumberg (1968) was probably somewhat over-optimistic in implying that all workers can play an important part in running industry, since he has only described the efforts of the more able minority. Although selection and other factors may have influenced the outcome, there is no evidence to suggest that many workers have been given control beyond their capacity in any programme of direct participation. Capacity therefore appears to have been a theoretical rather than a practical constraint, except where it has had an influence on the decision to participate.

2 Constraints determined by inclination

Our discussion of the role of capacity suggested that incli-nation may have a more significant impact on participative behaviour. Unfortunately, problems of measurement have inhibited extensive research and consequently a number of the comments in this section must be regarded as no more than tentative. Furthermore, while much of the research has implications for participation, participation was seldom the specific subject under investigation. One exception to this is some work examining the link between participation and personality.

One of the less publicized findings of the Lewin, Lippit and White (1939) study of leadership styles was the discovery that within groups of children there were marked individual differences in preferred leadership style. In particular, some children reacted positively to authoritarian leadership. The series of studies conducted by Adorno *et al* (1950) identified and measured 'the authoritarian personality' and sought its development in child rearing practices. Within this context, Sanford (1950) discovered that those with an authoritarian personality seem to prefer clearly defined hierarchical leadership and would therefore tend to respond negatively to participative situations.

Tannenbaum and Allport (1956) adopted some personality measures with the same population as that used by Morse and Reimer (1956) for their experiment. On the basis of the results, they matched the subjects to the programme which they were undergoing. Those whose personalities were congruent with the programme, whether it was authoritarian or participative in nature, were more satisfied with it and wanted it to last longer than those who were less well matched.

Vroom (1960) examined the hypothesis that "the relationship between psychological participation and both job satisfaction and job performance varied with the strength of the need for independence and the degree of authoritarianism" (Vroom 1964, p 118). Questionnaires were administered to a sample of 108 supervisors and various performance indices were also obtained. The results showed that the feeling of participating in decisions generally had a positive impact on attitudes and motivation. Highly authoritarian personalities were virtually unaffected by the opportunity to participate; those low on authoritarianism and with a high need for independence reacted most positively. Whilst this is an interesting study, it would be dangerous to generalize from it; the sample consisted of supervisors and not blue-collar workers and the study dealt with perceived rather than actual participation. Measures of objective participation did not appear to relate to each other or to anything else. Although this study highlights the potential importance of personality differences on the reaction to participation, it does no more than this.

Achievement motivation is one of the most relevant personality variables on which wide individual differences have been noted. McClelland (1961) has argued that individual differences can be attributed to variations in child rearing practices and more particularly to the emphasis placed on the need for success and social approval. This is of interest in the present context because McClelland argues that "Research has shown that individuals high in achievement tend to act in certain ways. For example, they prefer work situations where there is a challenge (moderate risk), concrete feedback on how well they are doing, and opportunity to take personal responsibility for achieving the work goals." (McClelland, 1965, quoted in Cummings and Scott, p 149).

Similar values could also be transmitted through religion (see Weber, 1930; Durkheim, 1951). Lenski (1961) has provided some empirical support for several of Weber's arguments. Among a sample from Detroit, he found that religious differences accounted for almost as much variation as class differences. White Protestants and Jews in blue-collar jobs had the traditional middle-class aspirations of the kind typified by high need achievement; by implication, they would have responded positively to a participative programme. In contrast, the Catholics were far more group-conscious and security centred.

A rather different perspective has been adopted by Korman (1970), who has produced evidence to suggest that it is mainly people with high self-esteem who strive to attain desirable goals. Because of their self-confidence and their strong belief in their own competence, they are more prepared to take action and more prepared to exert control. This could provide one interpretation of why those who are in more highly skilled jobs have often responded more positively to participative programmes than those who have previously exercised only minimal responsibility. This approach is only acceptable if low self-esteem really is an inhibitor of behaviour; it is possible to conceive of circumstances in which it could also be a stronger motivator.

A high level of self-esteem implies a readiness to take risks. This is an important element of a flexibility or versatility factor developed by Pym (1965) to examine acceptance of situations involving change and uncertainty. Changes in a footwear factory required machinists to make all types of footwear instead of a limited number of items. They were also given responsibility for quality inspection. At the same time, delays were cut to a minimum and piece-rates were improved. The machinists were divided into those who were high and low on flexibility, flexibility being measured by a 26-item questionnaire and an assessment of diversity of leisure interests. Although output levels of the two groups had been comparable before the change, for a long time afterwards the flexible group had a far higher level of output. It is possible that the groups varied not only in flexibility and desire for growth but also in self-esteem and in ability. This is one study in which competence does appear to have had an influence; nine out of the 99 operators left the job soon after the change, mainly because they were unable to cope with the new demands. A further 11 were still having difficulty 20 months after the change had taken place. Most but not all of these were in the security centred, less versatile group. It is unclear how far differing levels of competence determined these results, but it does seem that a personality factor influenced adaptability to a situation involving direct participation. To this extent, it highlights an important potential constraint.

Hackman and Lawler (1971) used a measure of what they

called 'higher order need-strength' to examine individual differences in reaction to job content. They found that it was a moderating variable in that those who obtained a high score on this measure, and therefore expressed a preference for jobs which satisfied intrinsic needs, responded positively to jobs with a high level of variety, autonomy and, to a lesser extent, feedback of performance. Those who scored lower on the measure of 'higher order need-strength' were less satisfied with jobs that had these attributes. This research is important for indicating differences in needs and aspirations relating to job content and therefore differences in satisfaction with a specific job content. The study notes these differences; it does not indicate why they should occur in the first place.

In this section we have examined a number of separate and often rather different 'personality' factors which could influence reaction to opportunities for direct participation. A number of them must be considered merely as theoretical constraints because little or no relevant research has been reported. Because they have usually been studied in isolation, the interrelationship between them is by no means clear. Attempts to look at sets of personality variables in relation to work motivation have generally proved unrewarding. Hackman (1969) for example managed to highlight the complexity of the task and reported wide individual differences but did little to further our understanding. Therefore although personality constraints undoubtedly operate, and must be recognized as influences on behaviour, our understanding of them remains limited.

The reaction to participation and to the opportunity for control can be influenced by previous experience other than that which is tied to personality. It can also influence the perception of what is meant by control. For example among railway workers, those who came from a rural farming background felt that station work offered little individual control because, in comparison with farm work, the timing of trains and the flow of passengers and parcels determined the pace of work. In contrast, ex-production line workers felt that they had an immense amount of control because they were no longer being dominated by machine-pacing. Similar differences were noted in the steel industry among those from various occupational backgrounds.

A failure to take account of background factors and previous experience contributed to the lack of success of the study by French, Israel and Aas (1957), which was intended to follow up the successful Coch and French (1948) change programme based upon group participation. The Norwegian workforce was accustomed to indirect participation through their representatives rather than the kind of direct participation in which everyone had a say; also, 64 per cent of them believed that piece-rates would be cut if they exceeded a certain standard rate of production. Not surprisingly, they treated a new approach to the raising of production levels with considerable suspicion.

Individual differences in some of the personality characteristics outlined earlier were attributed to child rearing practices and to the dissemination of values. The importance of early life on the development of attitudes towards participation has also been studied on a rural/urban dimension. Whyte (1955) reported a study by Dalton comparing the background characteristics of rate busters and restricters. Those who restricted output were the "sons of unskilled workers and grew up in large cities where for years they had been active in boys' gangs. Such activity tends to build loyalty to one's own group and opposition to authority – whether from parents or management" (Whyte, 1955, p 41). In contrast, the rate busters came either from a rural background or from a lower middle-class family. They tended to be loners with clear-cut aspirations to better their status. Summarizing the implications of this study, Whyte commented "The response to economic symbols is a learned response. It cannot be separated from other aspects of the individual's personal and social development. His responses will be conditioned by his relations with his family and community in the growing up process, by the status of his family and the drive for mobility that he does or does not learn in his earlier life, but the systems of belief on individualism versus group loyalty, on politics, and on the values of money that he learns in the course of his experience, and finally by the present pattern of social participation that he follows" (1955, p 48). In this statement, Whyte has extended the argument from social background right up to the immediate non-work social environment.

More recent work has been reported by Turner and Lawrence (1965), Blood and Hulin (1967) and Hulin and Blood (1968). In trying to measure the relationship between attitude and behaviour, Turner and Lawrence found a number of curvilinear relationships which led them to believe that they were dealing with at least two distinct populations. It emerged that the key variable was whether a factory was in a small town or in an urban setting. Blood and Hulin extended these findings to suggest that urban blue-collar workers were alienated from middle-class norms and therefore cannot be expected to conform to managerial initiatives. They can be contrasted with those from more rural backgrounds who seemed more disposed to accept middle class values.

Hulin and Blood have reviewed the relevant literature in relation to job enrichment. They conclude that the efficacy of job enrichment has been grossly overstated and that it is only likely to have a positive impact on those who have been reared in a rural or non-urban environment. As long as urban blue-collar workers are alienated from the middle-class values of management, they will be reluctant to accept controls which work towards managerial goals. Instead, they will prefer to use the opportunity for group control as a counter to management. Restrictive practices probably provide the best example of this. This work on the impact of geographical location was conducted in America, making it possible that the differences may be due to specific cultural factors. However an analysis of the location of some of the more successful change programmes involving direct participation, conducted by a number of companies in the United Kingdom, tends to lend circumstantial support to the wider application of this particular constraint. Wild (1970) has reported an exploratory study conducted in the United Kingdom which found variations in the attitudes of 2,543 unskilled female manual workers according to the density of population in the areas where they lived and worked.

3 *Constraints determined by circumstances*

Constraints of this type are different from constraints determined by inclination because they are the result of the circumstances in which an individual finds himself in relation to his environment. The most important item in this context is job level. A number of American researchers (see, for example, Friedmann and Honighurst, 1954; Morse and Weiss, 1955;) have examined the way in which individuals at various occupational levels view the world at work. The Morse and Weiss study comes closest to the kind of issues of concern in the present context. They found that those in middle class occupations valued the content and purpose of their work and the scope it gave them for accomplishment and the use of their skills. Those in working class occupations regarded work more in terms of labour, that is, as something to do, as a source of remuneration and as a means of passing the time and using their physical energy. Morse and Weiss noted that some of these differences could be accounted for by job content and by the background from which each individual came.

Kornhauser (1965) has noted that differences of attitude towards concepts of work can be found at different levels within the blue-collar group and Porter (1961) has described differences according to level among white-collar workers. It has also been possible to study changes in the attitudes of individuals who have moved from one group to another, generally as the result of a promotion. For example, after Lieberman (1956) had distributed an attitude survey, a number of the workforce were either promoted to foremen or appointed as shop stewards. These men were given the same questionnaire a year later; so too were two matched control groups. The foremen were found to have developed a management orientation while the shop stewards had become more pro-union. Some of the foremen were subsequently demoted, whereupon they re-adopted their original attitudes thus suggesting that occupational role, and the expectations associated with it, have an influence on attitudes towards work. The implications of research on job level is that the lower the level of the job, the less likely the incumbent is to express positive attitudes towards the concept of participation.

Moving further away from purely individual constraints, by broadening the concept of job level it becomes possible to view conflicting values in terms of class or work group solidarity. For instance, in Lockwood's (1966) discussion of sources of working class social imagery, he developed a theoretical model of a traditional proletarian worker. He felt that such a worker would see the world largely in the dichotomous terms of them and us, with 'us' unable to influence major decisions. This would necessitate a work group and class solidarity to combat and insulate himself against the behaviour of those in power. Anyone who reacted in this way would be likely to be suspicious of any moves initiated by management to introduce direct participation.

Nevertheless, worker reactions will vary in relation to changes in the social and economic environment. This process can be illustrated by the attitudes of unions and workpeople towards the idea of productivity bargaining. During the full employment of the late 1950s and early 1960s, the pressure was on management to use its workforce more efficiently. In these circumstances, where there was ample opportunity for the employment of displaced workers, the unions were prepared to bargain away many of their restrictive practices. Although this meant the loss of a certain amount of informal control, it often involved some sort of job enrichment or job enlargement (see Cotgrove, Dunhan and Vamplew, 1971; Daniel, 1970). With the rise of unemployment during the late 1960s, the willingness to bargain in this way rapidly diminished. From the time of the early Hawthorne studies, it has been demonstrated that smaller groups of workers will also seek control over factors influencing their job security during times of economic depression.

CONCLUSION

This brief review of some of the more important individual constraints on direct participation has emphasized their variety and potential significance. It is worth noting in this context that many of those who advocate direct participation, and job enrichment in particular, assume that there are no important differences in work motivation. It is also assumed that a high concern for job content is 'better' or 'more healthy' than a low concern. Such writers are, by implication, adopting a closed-system approach in which a job, rich in challenge, autonomy and variety, is the main source of fulfilment. The evidence on individual differences suggests that this is not the view held by many workers.

The chapter has also highlighted the sparsity of directly relevant research; much of the data we have used was not originally collected in the context of participation. Any conclusions must be regarded as very tentative. It does seem that constraints determined by capacity have sometimes been over-estimated and in practice those determined by inclination are probably more significant. This implies that it is the complexity of factors which go to make up an individual's orientation to his work, coupled with the circumstances of the job, and particularly level and experience of content, which account for significant individual differences. These individual differences are not necessarily constant; definitions of work can change and since those who have experience of participation generally welcome the idea of an extension of that participation, attitudes may gradually become more favourable. This is of significance to management in determining its policies in this area, for it indicates that it may be difficult to retreat from initial commitment. For whatever reason, workers who have extended experience of direct participation generally seek to retain the control that it provides.

Summary

This chapter examines the individual factors which influence the reaction to participative situations. Whereas organizational constraints determine the potential for participation, individual factors, usually arising outside the work environment, help to determine the likelihood that a worker will want to participate. Too many advocates of direct participation have failed to consider the nature or extent of individual differences. Partly as a result, little directly relevant research is available. Even surveys of attitudes towards participation have generally concentrated on indirect participation and have failed to analyse individual differences in depth. What evidence there is from such surveys suggests that skilled workers are likely to be more interested in participation than their less skilled colleagues, and that once workers have had some experience of participation they tend to want more. These two findings are almost the only ones to emerge consistently.

Most of the information on individual constraints is indirect evidence gleaned from studies of other subjects. These constraints can be divided into those determined by capacity, inclination and background circumstances. Capacity, defined in terms of level of skill and intelligence, consistently appears to influence participative behaviour, with the more skilled and intelligent reacting more favourably. On the other hand there is only slight evidence to indicate that, given the opportunity, individuals have been incapable of exerting direct control. Capacity would therefore seem to constitute a theoretical rather than a practical constraint.

Inclination has been most widely studied in terms of personality characteristics. There is a considerable body of evidence to indicate that those with flexible, non-authoritarian personalities are likely to have more favourable attitudes and to react more positively to direct participation. Other possibly interrelated variables which seem likely to influence reactions to participation include the need for achievement and level of self-esteem.

Among the individual background circumstances, age has not been shown to have a consistent relationship to types of participative behaviour. On the other hand it is not surprising to find that previous experience influences reactions; so too does an individual's cultural environment both in terms of an urban versus rural background and in terms of group identification. Those from a rural environment and with no strong feeling of working class solidarity seem more likely to respond favourably to direct participation.

NOTES

1 This was one of five alternative definitions, although combinations of definitions meant there were 11 possible alternatives. The only other one to attract more than a 10 per cent response was a combination of the above statement with 'workers share in profits and losses'; 12 per cent supported this definition.
2 Those with less schooling were also more likely to imagine that there would be positive personal gains, mainly of an economic nature, from participation.
3 For example, in 1971 ICI surveyed their total white-collar workforce on their attitudes towards unionization and other relevant features of the participative system.
4 This framework corresponds closely to that developed by Rodger (see Rodger and Cavanagh, 1968) which distinguishes capacity, inclination and background circumstances, primarily for the purpose of selection and vocational guidance.

CHAPTER TEN

CONCLUSION

The central purpose of this book has been to develop a framework for the analysis of worker participation and, within that framework, to evaluate the available evidence and to examine current thinking on the subject. We have concentrated upon what we have termed direct participation. It is direct in the sense that an individual is directly involved in decision making, rather than being involved through a representative. A number of reasons determined the decision to concentrate upon direct participation: much of the relevant data had been presented in a value-laden way and a model which could avoid this was needed; secondly, there had been a growing interest in certain forms of direct participation as a panacea for many of the human problems in industry. Associated with both these points, there has been considerable confusion over the objectives and the wider implications of direct participation.

Our analytic framework drew distinction on three dimensions. First, there was the distinction, relating to the type of participants, between direct and indirect participation. Secondly, distinctions could be made in terms of the content of participation; and thirdly, a variety of purposes of participation could be discerned. The tendency on the part of workers to participate will be primarily a function of the perceived gains from such action and their ability to control the situation so that they can obtain these gains. The expectancy model offers an explanation of the motivational issues involved but raises the question of the sort of rewards workers will value. The available evidence from within the United Kingdom indicates that workers are primarily interested in advancing or defending their pay, security and social relations. Although they admit to a concern for other aspects of their work, it is these three extrinsic factors which are of most importance.

A variety of forms of direct participation can be identified; in theory at least, they can be closely associated with different managerial ideologies. Nevertheless a common element is that each provides the worker with some control over his job content in terms either of what he does or, more usually, how he does it. Many managements have introduced various types of incentive payment schemes as a means of motivating and controlling the workforce. Yet these have the unintended consequence of providing the worker with control, and enabling him to determine his speed and sometimes the way in which he tackles his work. Occasionally workers will use this control to produce the results that management expected; often they will perceive that they have more to gain by restricting output to defend or increase the three important rewards mentioned above and they will act accordingly.

Increasing technological control has removed the logic in many incentive payment schemes since the worker can no longer determine the pace and sometimes not even the quality of his work. Some managers (Brown, 1962) have realized that such schemes are a major factor in loss of managerial control on the shop-floor and have managed to move on to alternative systems of payment. In many situations, incentive payment schemes will fail in their prime aim of improving productivity and will also provide a fertile ground for industrial relations conflicts. It would seem reasonable, therefore, to expect a decline in their use throughout industry. Whilst there does appear to have been a slow move away from them, they continue to exist widely not only in the United Kingdom but also in Sweden, for instance. Their popularity may be attributed in part to the failure of alternative payment systems to appear attractive to management. The costs of negotiating and implementing a changeover, when the workers are reluctant to lose their control, may be another factor. Finally, there may be hidden advantages, particularly in circumstances where there is a centrally controlled incomes policy, in retaining the flexibility provided by such schemes. Whatever the reasons, it seems likely that they will continue to provide many workers with an important means of direct control over their jobs.

Human relations policies, whilst permitting an extension of direct control, seldom result in such a tangible form of control as that presented by incentive payment schemes. For management, democratic leadership, open communication and work group participation in change have the potential to achieve all four of the major objectives of participation, namely increased productivity, increased job satisfaction, improved industrial relations and greater industrial democracy. From the workers' point of view, the gains to be had are usually perceived as marginal. It would be fair to say that there has often been an increase in overall job satisfaction and occasionally industrial conflict may have been lessened. But productivity has seldom improved except indirectly, through reductions in absenteeism or labour turnover. For many people, these strategies represent a sophisticated means of eliciting worker cooperation. While many workers will welcome the removal of authoritarian control, the additional control accruing to them will not often be sufficient to influence significantly their most valued rewards; the worker response, therefore, will often be one of apathy.

The third main category of direct participation exists under a variety of titles such as job enrichment, autonomous work groups and work structuring; essentially it is concerned with the re-design of jobs to provide greater autonomy, responsibility and scope for achievement. Again, from management's point of view, this approach could potentially meet all four objectives of participation. The data we have analysed has been inconclusive. The overwhelming majority of reported studies has indicated certain improvements in productivity but it has generally been impossible to specify with any confidence the cause of these improvements. This is because a number of interrelated changes have generally taken place at the same time, so that re-design of the jobs has been associated with the introduction of new machinery, the implementation of method study or a reorganization of the system of payment. The only attempt at a controlled experiment was not completed, but lasted long enough to indicate that job enrichment alone was not always going to be accepted by shop-floor workers (Paul, 1969). The inability to control the variety of intervening variables – and the lack of control groups of any sort – has been a serious limitation to much of the evaluative work in this as in many other types of behavioural research in industry. Enough evidence has accumulated to indicate that the introduction of job enrichment, in isolation and viewed primarily as a motivational strategy, is often unlikely to succeed. In fact the way in which the change is introduced seems to be a critical determinant of its success.

The importance attached to the process of change is significant for two reasons: first for what it tells us about workers' priorities and about their reactions in relation to these priorities; and secondly because of its implications for managers who are seeking to introduce direct, or even new forms of indirect participation. Returning to the first point, workers will resist any attempts to impose unfamiliar, and hence unpredictable change or changes from which they are not certain that they will benefit. Management may sometimes be able to overcome this by introducing a change in the content of jobs along with more conventional changes of a type we have described. Usually, the workers will seek to channel such changes through the collective bargaining process. In this way collective bargaining remains the most significant form of participation. Such an approach fits into the concepts developed by McCarthy and Ellis (1973) who argue that it is in management's interests to allow workers to become involved in all aspects of decision-making and to do so mainly through collective bargaining. Within this context job enrichment, worker directors and other forms of participation can make a useful but essentially secondary contribution. This emphasis is not dissimilar to the current thinking of many trade unionists in the United Kingdom.

In many respects it is not surprising that management faces opposition when introducing forms of direct participation, and more especially forms such as job enrichment and autonomous work groups which will be less familiar to the worker. One reason is that moves to introduce direct participation almost invariably come from management; only with incentive payment schemes, and then only occasionally, have workers taken the initiative. In a conventional industrial relations context, a suggestion from management that workers should accept something which is unfamiliar but apparently in their interests can be expected to be met with scepticism. For such changes to be introduced, a sophisticated strategy is required.

In contrast to the unfamiliarity and uncertainty of job enrichment and autonomous work groups, workers have felt that collective bargaining is well tried and useful and they are continually putting pressure on management to see it extended. In favouring this one form of indirect participation, they have concentrated on it rather than seeking alternatives. Attempts to channel their enthusiasm into joint consultation met with some initial success but this fell off when workers realized that it side-tracked them from what they considered to be the most important issues. Despite the apparent success of supervisory boards and works councils in certain sections of European industry, they have also met with widespread scepticism and apathy. Previous experience, coupled with evidence from reaction to the worker directors in the British Steel Corporation, suggests that attitudes among workers in the United Kingdom would be at best similar and possibly considerably more negative. We would therefore share the misgivings of the Confederation of British Industry and the Trades Union Congress about the value of an imposition of such schemes by the European Economic Community.

What, then, is management to do? As McCarthy and Ellis (1973) have suggested, faced with pressures from below and with pressures from without, including increasing Governmental regulation and a growing debate on the quality of working life, management seems likely to look increasingly to the possibilities of job design both as a technique and as a means of maintaining its legitimacy. Pressure from the workers means that this cannot be viewed in isolation. The available evidence points to certain strategies which can both facilitate change and increase the chances of these changes being successful. From a theoretical point of view, as we suggested in chapter 8, this would seem to require an analysis which combines an action frame of reference with a socio-technical systems approach. The socio-technical approach points to the need for careful preparation and more particularly a detailed analysis of the technical, social, information and payment systems. Apart from the obvious objective of assessing the implications and determining the potential nature of the change, this will point to the need to set up discreet units of production and to remove constraints on their effective operation. The action frame of reference will show how the workers are likely to view the change and, as already indicated, will often point to the wisdom of introducing it in the context of a conventional change, such as technological innovation and through the familiar means of collective bargaining. This implies that changes based on strategies associated with Herzberg's motivator-hygiene theory, which tend to view job content in isolation, and which are essentially non-participative, are unlikely to succeed.

Evidence from studies of successful changes in job design indicate the value of involving worker representatives in the planning of change and of being completely open with them about any repercussions. With this in mind, the change is facilitated if long-term grievances over issues such as pay and security can be cleared up in advance. Because of the need for extensive preparation and negotiation a lengthy time perspective is required; and because of the difficulties of going back on a change of this type, and in view of the risks involved, it is essential to have the commitment of top management and highly desirable to have a parallel commitment from senior workers' representatives. Finally, returning to the socio-technical implications, it is unlikely that a one-off change will be either totally successful or sufficient in itself; it may therefore be more useful to think in terms of a series of changes. This in turn can place a considerable strain on management and union resources and implies careful planning and training. Changes of the type envisaged are likely to have possibly unforeseen repercussions on people such as supervisors and middle managers, who may feel that their positions are threatened. In the end, what may emerge can look like a productivity bargain; it is not surprising to find that many of the better known productivity bargains, perhaps unintentionally, contain elements of job enrichment or autonomous work groups.

Clearly each case will have its individual characteristics and therefore there will be no standard approach which will always succeed. What we have tried to show in the preceding paragraphs is that management's chances of success in introducing this particular form of direct participation can be enhanced if their technical approach is sound and if they take full account of the needs and attitudes of the workers. This means that these alternative forms of participation should in no way be seen as substitutes for collective bargaining.

It is important not to overlook the constraints upon direct participation through job design. From the worker's point of view, the various constraints can be explained within the expectancy model. In other words, there will be different ways in which the potential of a participative situation is perceived. Management must take account of these individual differences and in addition has a further set of constraints to consider. These are concerned with aspects of organizational structure and in particular with the nature of the technology. The control systems and the predictability inherent in many modern technical systems limit the amount of freedom available to the worker and the financial risks involved as a result of damage to machinery, loss of production and confusion over planning will not always be seen to be justified. Since technological developments appear to limit the potential for direct participation, the question arises of whether they are reversible. The evidence from some of the more recent continental efforts at work structuring, with a focus on autonomous work groups rather than individual job enrichment, suggests that only a few companies are as yet prepared to accept the risks involved.

In this final chapter we have suggested that, for technical reasons, management is likely to be forced to pay more attention to direct participation through job enrichment and autonomous work groups rather than through other forms. Such policies can also serve legitimatory functions by helping to channel attention away from contentious issues. Certainly, there is an element of legitimacy in attempts to strike a bargain by apparently extending workers' control at the same time as giving them higher wages, when in fact this control may be somewhat limited. What some managers may have failed to consider is that there is evidence to suggest that experience of this and some other types of participation begets the desire for more.

It is difficult to accept that the goals of management will often be compatible with the outcomes likely to be associated with a considerable extension of direct participation. Taken to its logical extreme, such an extension would almost certainly present pressure for a reversal of technological trends; initially a socio-technical systems concept might be able to account for this but a continued trend would require a greater emphasis than at any time since the industrial revolution on social satisfactions. Although there is little evidence in the United Kingdom that workers would want to go to this extreme, it does indicate that it would be dangerous to assume a continued value consensus over outcomes between management and workers. Our evidence that workers retain a primary concern for pay and security would seem, in many circumstances, to support this view. Yet such an assumption is tacitly built into most

225

participative models, particularly those associated with job design. Assumptions about a value consensus also ignore the evidence that the orientations to work of both workers and managers can be redefined as a result of experience. Given that this is so, there can be no reliance upon a constant set of objectives particularly if, in the case of the workers, these are likely to relate to needs external to the organization and are therefore largely beyond the control of management.

The line of argument we have developed is dependent upon the continuance of a profit and growth oriented consumer society. Such a society puts pressure on industry to continue technological trends towards automation and encourages the worker to continue to see work as a means to an end. To some extent, the worker can still be seen to sell his labour to the highest bidder. This concept has limitations because it begs the question of what he sells his labour for. There is no doubt that money is the prime concern; but security is also important, as are the right social conditions.

Taking this a step further it is possible to conceive of the worker selling his marginal labour for intrinsic job satisfaction. With any growth in marginal labour or any slackening in the consumer society, the worker's orientations could change to provide a more favourable view of direct participation. Evidence is beginning to accumulate to suggest that this is happening in a number of countries.

It should be apparent that the situation as it affects direct participation is unstable and subject to constant redefinition. The critical variables would seem to be the values and goals of society. In the United Kingdom at present, there is ample evidence of a conflict of values over the distribution of wealth and power. In so far as direct participation implicitly seeks to maintain the *status quo* and to divest interest to the intrinsic rather than the extrinsic rewards, it can be seen partly as a device for sophisticated social management. In this case, its contribution to social harmony and management efficiency is likely to be minimal mainly because, as we have seen, workers will refuse to accept it in isolation without attention also being paid to what they consider to be more relevant issues. Where these issues can be taken into account, its chances of success are greater.

By now, it is apparent that the ideological content of the more popular current forms of direct participation places them alongside other schemes of management designed to obtain greater cooperation from the worker. Judged as a style of management, it appears to be successful only under the conditions outlined earlier. But what so clearly emerges is that direct participation is not a panacea: its potential must be comprehensively analysed to take account of the constraints of organizational structure and individual motivation. Our analysis has sought to emphasize that advocates of direct participation have often failed to take account of significant variables. We have tried to bring these variables to the attention of the reader.

BIBLIOGRAPHY

ADORNO, T W, FRENKEL-BRUNSWIK, E, LEVINSON, D J, and SANFORD, R N, *The Authoritarian Personality*, Harper, 1950, New York

ANDERSON, P, 'The Limits and Possibilities of Trade Union Action' in Blackburn, R, and Cockburn, A, (eds) *The Incompatibles: Trade Union Militancy and The Consensus*, Penguin, 1967

ANTHONY, P D, *Joint Consultation—Its Meaning and Purpose in a Nationalised Industry*, MSc Thesis (unpublished), University of Wales, 1969

ARGYLE, M, 'The relay assembly test-room in retrospect', *Occupational Psychology*, 27, 98–103, 1953

ARGYLE, M, GARDNER, G, and CIOFFI, F, 'Supervisory methods related to productivity, absenteeism and labour turnover', *Human Relations*, 11, 23–40, 1958

ARGYRIS, C, *Personality and the Organization: The Conflict Between System and the Individual*, Harper, 1957, New York

ARGYRIS, C, *Integrating the Individual and the Organization*, Wiley, 1964, New York

ASCH, S E, 'Studies of independence and conformity: A minority of one against a unanimous majority', *Psychological Monographs*, 70, No 9, 1956

BAKKE, E W, *The Unemployed Man*, Nisbet, 1933, New York

BALDAMUS, W, *Efficiency & Effort*, Tavistock Publications, 1961

BANKS, J A, *Industrial Participation. Theory and Practice: A Case Study*, Liverpool University Press, 1963

BEHREND HILDE, 'The effort-bargain', *Industrial & Labour Relations Review*, 10, 503–15, 1957

BELL, D, *The End of Ideology*, Collier, 1961, New York

BENDIG, A W, and STILLMAN, E L, 'Dimensions of job

incentives among college students', *J of Applied Psychology*, 42, 367–71, 1958

BENDIX, R, *Work and Authority in Industry*, Wiley, 1956, New York

BENNIS, W G, *Changing Organizations*, McGraw-Hill, 1966, New York

BEYNON, H, *Working for Ford*, Penguin, 1973

BISHOP, T, 'When workers take control', *Personnel Management*, 1973

BLAKE, R R, and MOUTON, J J, *The Managerial Grid*, Gulf Publishing Co, 1964, Houston

BLAUNER, R, *Alienation and Freedom: The Factory Worker and his Industry*, University of Chicago Press, 1964, Chicago

BLOOD, M R, and HULIN, C L, 'Alienation, environmental characteristics and worker responses', *J of Applied Psychology*, 51, 284–90, 1967

BLUMBERG, P, *Industrial Democracy: The Sociology of Participation*, Constable, 1968

BRANNEN, P, BATSTONE, E, FATCHETT, D, and WHITE, P, *Summary of Research Report*, British Steel, 1972

BROWN, J A C, *The Social Psychology of Industry*, Penguin, 1954

BROWN, R, and BRANNEN, P, 'Social relations and social perspectives amongst shipbuilding workers', *Sociology*, IV, 1 and 2, 1970

BROWN, R, BRANNEN, P, COUSINS, J, and SAMPHIER, M, in SMITH, M A, PARKER, S, and SMITH, C, (eds) *Leisure and Society in Britain*, Allen Lane, 1973

BROWN, W, *Piecework Abandoned*, Heinemann, 1962

BUITER, J H, 'Production standards, financial incentives and the reaction of workers', *Work Study and Management*, 8, 354–62, 1964

BURNS, T, and STALKER, G M, *The Management of Innovation*, Tavistock Publications, 1961

CAREY, A, 'The Hawthorne Studies: a radical criticism', *American Sociological Review*, 32, 403–16, 1967

CHADWICK-JONES, J, *Automation and Behaviour*, John Wiley, 1969

CHILD, J, *British Management Thought*, Allen & Unwin, 1969

CHILD, J, *The Business Enterprise in Modern Industrial Society,* Collier-MacMillan, 1969

CLARKE, R O, FATCHETT, D J, and ROBERTS, B C, *Workers Participation in Management in Britain,* Heinemann, 1973

CLARKE, R O, and FATCHETT, D J, 'Workers Participation in Management in Great Britain', *International Institute for Labour Studies Bulletin,* No 9, 1972, Geneva

CLEGG, H, *A New Approach to Industrial Democracy,* Blackwell, 1960

COATES, K, and TOPHAM, A, *Industrial Democracy in Great Britain,* MacGibbon & Lee, 1968

COCH, L, and FRENCH, J R P, 'Overcoming resistance to change', *Human Relations,* 1, 512–32, 1948

CORNER, D C, 'Financial Incentives in the Smaller Business', *Occasional Papers in Social and Economic Administration,* 5, Edutext Publications, 1967

COTGROVE, S, DUNHAM, J, and VAMPLEW, C, *The Nylon Spinners: a case study in productivity bargaining and job enlargement,* Allen & Unwin, 1971

COUSINS, J, 'The Non-Militant Shop Steward', *New Society,* 3 February 1972

CROSLAND, C A R, *The Conservative Enemy,* Cape, 1962

CUMMINGS, L L, and SCOTT, W G, *Readings in Organizational Behaviour and Human Performance,* Irwin, 1969, Homewood, Ill

DANIEL, W W, *Beyond the Wage-Work Bargain,* PEP, 1970

DAVIS, L E and TAYLOR J C, *Design of Jobs,* Penguin, 1972

DAY, R C, and HAMBLIN, R L, 'Some effects of close and punitive styles of supervision', *American J of Sociology,* 69, 499–510, 1964

DRUCKER, P F, *The Practice of Management,* Harper, 1954

EILON, S, 'Problems in Studying Management', *International Journal of Production Research,* 1, No 4, 1962

ELDRIDGE, J E T, *Sociology and Industrial Life,* Michael Joseph, 1971

Electrical Trades Union, 'Evidence to Royal Commission on Trade Unions and Employees Associations', *Minutes of Evidence,* 57, 2469, HMSO, 1966

EMERY, F E, 'Democratisation of the Workplace (an historical review of studies)', *TIHR Doc T813*, 1966

EMERY, F E, THORSRUD, E, in co-operation with TRIST, E, *Form and Content in Industrial Democracy*, Tavistock Publications, 1969

FELDMAN, H, *Problems in Labour Relations*, Macmillan, 1937, New York

FIEDLER, F E *A Theory of Leadership Effectiveness*, McGraw-Hill, 1967, New York

FLANAGAN, J C, 'The critical incident technique', *Psychological Bulletin*, 51, 327–58, 1954

FLANDERS, A, *The Fawley Productivity Agreements*, Faber, 1964

FLANDERS, A, SLOAN, N, and TAYLOR, D, 'Productivity Bargaining', *Steel Review*, p 43, 5–8, 1966

FLANDERS, A, POMERANZ, R, and WOODWARD, J, *Experiment in Industrial Democracy: a study of the John Lewis Partnership*, Faber, 1968

FLEISHMAN, E A, 'The description of supervisory behaviour', *J of Applied Psychology*, 37, 1–6, 1953

FLEISHMAN, E A, HARRIS, E F, and BURTT, N E, *Leadership and Supervision in Industry*, Bureau of Educational Research, Ohio State University, 1955

FORD, R N, *Motivation Through the Work Itself*, American Management Association, 1969, New York

FOX, A, *A Sociology of Work in Industry*, Collier-Macmillan, 1971

FRENCH, J R P, Jr, 'Field Experiments: Changing Group Productivity' in MILLER, J G, (ed) *Experiments in Social Process: A Symposium on Social Psychology*, McGraw-Hill, 1950, New York

FRENCH, J R P, JR, ISRAEL, J, and ÅS, D, 'An experiment on participation in a Norwegian factory, *Human Relations*, 13, 3–19, 1960

FRIEDMANN, E A, and HAVINGHURST, R J, *The Meaning of Work and Retirement*, Chicago University Press, 1954, Chicago

FRIEDRICKS, R W, 'Dialetical Sociology: towards a resolution of the current crisis in Western Sociology', *Brit J of Sociology*, XXIII, 3, 1972

FÜRSTENBERG, F, 'Workers Participation in Management in the Federal Republic of Germany', *International Institute for Labour Studies, Bulletin*, 6, 1969

GANTT, H L, *Organizing for Work*, George Allen and Unwin, 1919

GENNARD, J, and ROBERTS, B, 'Trends in Plant and Company Bargaining', *Scot. J. of Political Economy*, June 1970

GOLDTHORPE, J H, and LOCKWOOD, D, 'Affluence and the British class structure', *Sociological Rev.*, II, 2, 1963

GOLDTHORPE, J H, LOCKWOOD, D, BECKHOFER, F, and PLATT, J, *The Affluent Worker: Industrial Attitudes and Behaviour*, CUP, 1968

GOODRICH, C L, *The Frontiers of Control: A Study in British Workshop Relations*, Bell, 1920

GOTTING, D A, 'The Introduction of a wage grading and productivity plan in a large engineering firm', *Brit J of Industrial Relations*, IX, 3, 1971

Government Social Survey, *Workplace Industrial Relations*, HMSO, 1968

GRAHAM, D, and SLUCKIN, W, 'Different kinds of reward as industrial incentives', *Research Rev, Durham*, 5, 54–56, 1954

GUEST, D, *Job Design and Work Motivation* (To be published by Penguin, 1975)

HACKMAN, R C, *The Motivated Working Adult*, American Management Association, 1969, New York

HACKMAN, J R, and LAWLER, E E III, 'Employee reactions to job characteristics', *J. of Applied Psychology*, 55, 259–65, 1971. Abbreviated version reprinted in DAVIS, L E, and TAYLOR, J C, *Design of Jobs*, Penguin, 1972

HEMPHILL, J K, 'Job descriptions for executives', *Harvard Business Review*, 37, 55–67, 1959

HERZBERG, F, *Work and the Nature of Man*, World Publishing Co, 1966, Cleveland

HERZBERG, F, MAUSNER, B, PETERSON, R, and CAPWELL, D, *Job Attitudes: Review of Research and Opinion*, Psychological Services of Pittsburgh, 1957

HERZBERG, F, MAUSNER, B, and SNYDERMAN, G, *The Motivation to Work,* Wiley, 1959, New York

HESPE, G W A, and LITTLE, A J, 'Some aspects of employee participation' in WARR, P, (ed) *Psychology at work,* Penguin, 1971

HICKSON, D J, 'Worker choice of payment system', *Occupational Psychology,* 37, 93–100, 1963

HILGENDORF, E L, and IRVING, B L, *Worker Participation in Management: a study of the Attitudes of British Rail Employees,* unpublished Report No HRC461 of the Tavistock Institute of Human Relations, 1970

HILL, P, *Towards a New Philosophy of Management,* Gower Press, 1971

HININGS, C R, and LEE, G, 'Decisions of organisation structure and their context: A replication, *Sociology,* 5, 1, 1971

HINTON, B L, 'An empirical investigation of the Herzberg methodology and two-factor theory', *Organizational Behaviour & Human Performance,* 3, 286–309, 1968

HOLTER, H, 'Attitudes towards employee participation in company decision making processes', *Human Relations,* 18, 297–321, 1965

HOUSE, R J, and WIGDOR, L A, 'Herzberg's dual factor theory of job satisfaction and motivation: A review of evidence and a criticism', *Personnel Psychology,* 20, 369–89, 1967

HULIN, C L, and BLOOD, M R, 'Job enlargement, individual differences and worker responses', *Psychological Bulletin,* 69, 41–55, 1968

HYMAN, R, *Strikes,* Fontana, 1972

INCOMES DATA, *Report No 96,* August 1970

INDIK, B P, 'Some effects of organization size on member attitudes and behaviour', *Human Relations,* 16, 1963

Industrial Relations Counsellors Inc, 'Group wage incentives: experience with the Scanlon Plan', *New York Magazine,* 18–40, 1962, and in LUPTON, T, (ed) *Payment Systems,* Penguin, 1972

INGHAM, G, *Size of Industrial Organization and Worker Behaviour,* CUP, 1970

Institution of Works Managers, 'Survey on Incentive Payments: first report findings', *Works Management,* May 1966

JACKSON, J M, 'The effects of changing the leadership of small work groups', *Human Relations,* 6, 25–44, 1953

JACOBSON, E, *Foreman-steward participation practices and worker attitudes in a unionized factory,* unpublished doctoral dissertation, University of Michigan, 1951, Ann Arbor

JANSON, R, 'Job Enrichment in Modern Office' in MAHER, J R, (ed) *New Perspectives in Job Enrichment,* Van Nostrand Reinhold, 1971

JAQUES, E, *Equitable Payment,* Heinemann, 1961

JURGENSEN, C E, 'What job applicants look for in a company', *Personnel Psychology,* 1, 433–45, 1948

KATZ, D, MACCOBY, N, GURIN, G, and FLOOR, L, *Productivity, Supervision and Morale among Railroad Workers,* Institute for Social Research, 1951, Ann Arbor, Mich

KATZ, D, MACCOBY, N, and MORSE, N C, *Productivity, Supervision and Morale in an Office Situation,* Part 1, Institute for Social Research, 1950, Ann Arbor, Mich

KERR, C, DUNLOP, J T, HARBIN, F H, and MYERS, C A, *Industrialism and Industrial Man,* Heinemann, 1964

KING, N, 'Clarification and evaluation of the two-factor theory of job satisfaction', *Psychological Bulletin,* 74, 18–31, 1970

KING TAYLOR, L, *Not for Bread Alone,* Business Books Ltd, 1972

KNOWLES, H P, and SAXBERG, B O, 'Human relations and the nature of man', *Harvard Business Review,* March-April, 23–39, 172–78, 1967

KOLAJA, J, *Workers Councils: The Yugoslav Experience,* Tavistock Publications, 1965

KORMAN, A K, ' "Consideration", "initiating structure", and organizational criters—a review', *Personnel Psychology* 19, 349–61, 1966

KORMAN, A K, 'Towards a hypothesis of work behaviour', *J. of Applied Psychology,* 54, 31–41, 1970

KORNHAUSER, A, *Mental Health of the Industrial Worker,* Wiley, 1965, New York

Labour Party, *Industrial Democracy,* Labour Party, 1967

LAMMERS, C J, 'Power and participation in decision making in formal organizations', *Amer J of Sociology,* 73, No. 2, September 1967

LANDSBERGER, H A, *Hawthorne Revisited,* Cornell University Press, 1958, Ithica, NY

LAWLER, E E, 'Job design and employee motivation', *Personnel Psychology,* 22, 426–35, 1969

LAWLER, E E, *Pay and Organizational Effectiveness: a psychological view,* McGraw-Hill, 1971, New York

LEWIN, K, *The Conceptual Representation and Measurement of Psychological Forces,* Duke University Press, 1938, Durham, N. Carolina

LEWIN, K, LIPPITT, R, and WHITE, R K, 'Patterns of aggressive behaviour in experimentally created social climates', *J of Social Psychology,* 10, 271–99, 1939

LIEBERMAN, S, 'The effect of changes in role on the attitudes of occupants', *Human Relations,* 9, 485–502, 1956

LIKERT, R, *New Patterns of Management,* McGraw-Hill, 1961, New York

LIKERT, R, *The Human Organization: Its Management and Value,* McGraw-Hill, 1967, New York

LOCKWOOD, D, 'Sources of variation in working class images of society', *Sociological Review,* 14, 3, 1966

LOWIN, A, and CRAIG, J R, 'The influence of level of performance on managerial style: an experimental object-lesson in the ambiguity of correlational data', *Organizational Behaviour and Human Performance,* 3, 440–58, 1968

LUPTON, T, *On the Shop Floor,* Pergamon Press, 1963

McCARTHY, W E J, 'The Role of Shop Stewards in British Industry', *Royal Commission on Trade Unions and Employees Associations,* Research Papers No 1, HMSO, 1966

McCARTHY, W E J, and ELLIS, N D, *Management by Agreement,* Hutchinson, 1973

McCARTHY, W E J, and PARKER, J R, 'Shop stewards and workshop relations', *Royal Commission on Trade Unions and Employer's Associations,* Research Papers 10, HMSO, 1968

McCLELLAND, D C, *The Achieving Society,* Van Nostrand, 1961, New Jersey

McCLELLAND, D C, 'Achievement motivation can be developed', *Harvard Business Review,* 43, 6–14, 20–23, 178, 1965

McGREGOR, D, *The Human Side of Enterprise,* McGraw-Hill, 1960, New York

MACCOBY, E E, NEWCOMB, T W, and HARTLEY, E L, (eds) *Readings in Social Psychology,* 3rd edn, Henry Holt, 1958

MACKENZIE DAVEY, D, ROCKINGHAM GILL, D, and McDONNELL, P, *Attitude Surveys in Industry,* IPM, 1970

MAHER, J, OVERBAGH, W, PALMER, G, and PIERSOL, D, 'Enriched jobs improve inspection', *Work Study & Management Services,* 14(10), 821–24, 1970

MALLET, S, *La Nouvelle Class Ouvrière,* Editions du Seuil, 1963, Paris

MANGHAM, I, SHAW, S, and WILSON, D, 'How to organize development', *Management Today,* 88–91, 138, September 1971

MANN, F C, *A study of work satisfactions as a function of the discrepancy between inferred aspirations and achievement,* unpublished doctoral dissertation, University of Michigan, 1953, Ann Arbor

MARCH, J G, and SIMON, H A, *Organizations,* Wiley, 1958, New York

MARCUSE, H, *One-Dimensional Man,* Routledge, 1964

MARRIOTT, R, *Incentive Payment Systems,* 3rd rev edn, Staples Press, 1968

MARSH, A I, and COKER, E E, 'Shop Steward Organization in the Engineering Industry', *Brit J of Industrial Relations,* 1, June 1963

MARSH, A I, and McCARTHY, W J, 'Disputes Procedures in Britain', Part 2, *Royal Commission on Trade Unions and Employers Associations,* Research Papers No 2, Part 2, HMSO, 1968

MARX, K, and ENGELS, F, *The German Ideology,* Laurence & Wishart, 1965

MASLOW, A H, 'A theory of human motivation', *Psychological Review,* 50, 370–96, 1943

MASLOW, A H, *Eupsychian Management: A Journal,* Irwin-Dorsey, 1965, Homewood, Ill

MAYO, E, *Human Problems of an Industrial Civilisation,* Macmillan, 1933, New York

MECHANIC, D, 'Sources of power of low participants in complex organizations', *Administrative Science Quarterly,* 7. 349–64, 1962

MICHELS, R, *Political Parties,* Collier, 1962

MILLS, C W, 'The contributions of sociology to studies of industrial relations', *Proceedings of the First Annual Meeting of the Industrial Relations Research Association,* 212–13, 1948

MILLS, C W, *White Collar,* OUP, 1956, New York

MORSE, N C, and WEISS, R J, 'The function and meaning of work and the job', *Am Sociological Review,* 20, 191–98, 1955

MORSE, N C, and REIMER, E, 'The experimental change of a major organizational variable', *J of Abnormal & Social Psychology,* 52, 120–29, 1956

MUENCH, G A, 'A clinical psychologist's treatment of labor-management conflicts', *Personal Psychology,* 13, 165–72, 1960

MUENCH, G A, 'A clinical psychologist's treatment of labor-management conflicts: A four-year study', *J. of Human Psychology,* 1, 92–97, 1963

MUMFORD, E, and BANKS, O, *The Computer and the Clerk,* Routledge, 1967

MYERS, M S, 'Who are your motivated workers?', *Harvard Business Rev.,* 42, 73–88, 1964

National Board for Prices and Incomes, *Productivity Agreements,* Report 123, HMSO, 1969

National Institute for Industrial Psychology, *Joint Consultation in British Industry,* Staples Press, 1952

NEAL, L F, and ROBERTSON, A, *The Manager's Guide to Industrial Relations,* Allen & Unwin, 1968

NEULOH, O, *Der Neue Betriebstil,* Tübingen, 1960

NICHOLS, T, *Ownership, Control and Ideology,* Allen & Unwin, 1969

Opinion Research Corporation, *'Productivity' from the Worker's Standpoint,* ORC, 1949, Princeton, NJ

OPSAHL, R L, and DUNNETTE, M D, 'The role of financial compensation in industrial motivation', *Psychological Bulletin,* 66, No. 2, 94–118, 1960

OWEN-SMITH, E, *Productivity Bargaining,* Pan Piper, 1971

PARKER, S R, 'Work and Non-Work in Three Occupations', *Sociological Review,* 13, No 1, 1965

PARKER, S R, *The Future of Work and Leisure,* MacGibbon & Kee, 1971

PARKER, S R, BROWN, R K, CHILD, J, and SMITH, M A, *The Sociology of Industry,* Allen & Unwin, 1967

PAUL, W J, and ROBERTSON, K B, *Learning from Job Enrichment,* report issued by Central Personnel Dept. of Imperial Chemical Industries Ltd, 1969

PAUL, W J, and ROBERTSON, K, *Job Enrichment and Employee Motivation,* Gower Press, 1970

PHILIPS LTD, *Work-structuring: a summary of experiments at Philips,* 1963–1968, NV Philips' Gloeilampenfabrieken, 1969, Eindhoven, Holland

PORTER, L W, 'A study of perceived need satisfactions in bottom and middle management jobs', *J of Applied Psychology,* 45, 1–10, 1961

PORTER, L W, 'Job attitudes in management: I perceived deficiencies in need fulfilment as a function of job level', *J of Applied Psychology,* 46, 375–84, 1962

PORTER, L W, 'Job attitudes in management: II. perceived importance of needs as a function of job level', *J. of Applied Psychology,* 47, 141–48, 1963

PORTER, L W, and LAWLER, E E, *Managerial Attitudes and Performance,* Dorsey-Irwin, 1968, Homewood, Ill

PUGH, D S, HICKSON, D J, HININGS, C R, and TURNER, C, 'The context of organization structures', *Administrative Science Quarterly,* 14, No. 1, March 1969

PUTNAM, M L, 'Improving Employee relations', *Personnel Journal,* 8, 314–25, 1930

PYM, D, 'Is there a future for wage incentive systems?' *Brit J of Industrial Relations,* 2, 379–97, 1964

239

RADKE, M, and KLISURICH, D, 'Experiments in changing food habits', *Journal of the American Diet Association,* 23, 403–09, 1947

RAMELSON, B, 'The possibilities and limitation of workers control', *The Debate on Workers Control,* Institute for Workers Control, 1970, Nottingham

REDDIN, W J, *Managerial Effectiveness,* McGraw-Hill, 1970, New York

REIF, W C, and SCHODERBEK, P P, 'Job Enlargement: antidote to apathy', *Management of Personnel Quarterly,* 1960, 5, 16–23, 1966. Also in McFARLAND, D E, (ed) *Personnel Management,* Penguin, 1971

RHENMAN, E, *Co-operation and Conflict in Organizations,* John Wiley, 1970

RICHARDSON, F L W, and WALKER, C R, *Human Relations in an Expanding Company,* Yale University, 1948, New Haven, Conn

ROBERTS, B C, *Trade Union Government and Administration,* Bell, 1956

ROBERTS, B C, LOVERIDGE, R, and JENNARD, J, *The Reluctant Militants,* Heinemann, 1972

ROBERTS, G, 'Demarcation Rules in Shipbuilding and Ship Repairing', *Occasional Paper, No. 14, Dept. of Applied Economics, Cambridge,* CUP, 1967

ROETHLISBERGER, F J, and DICKSON, W J, *Management and the Worker,* Harvard University Press, 1939, Cambridge, Mass

ROMMETVEIT, R, *Social Norms and Roles: Explorations in the psychology of enduring social pressures,* The University of Minnesota Press, 1955, Minneapolis

ROSEN, N A, *Leadership Change and Work-Group Dynamics,* Staples, 1970

ROSS, I C, and ZANDER, A, 'Need satisfactions and employee turnover', *Personnel Psychology,* 10, 327–38, 1957

ROY, D, 'Quota restrictions and gold-bricking in a machine shop', *Am J of Sociology,* 57, 427–42, 1952

ROY, D, 'Efficiency and "the fix": informal intergroup relations in a piece-work machine shop', *Am J of Sociology,* 60, 255–66, 1955

Royal Commission on Trade Unions and Employers Associations, Report, Cmnd 3623, HMSO, 1968

Royal Commission on Trade Unions and Employers Associations, 'Productivity bargaining & restrictive practices', *Royal Commission on Trade Unions and Employers Associations*, Research Papers 4, HMSO, 1967

SALES, S, 'Supervisory style and productivity: a review', *Personnel Psychology*, 19, 275–86, 1966

SANFORD, F H, *Authoritarianism and Leadership*, Institute for Research in Human Relations, 1950, Philadelphia

SAYLES, L, *Behaviour of Industrial Work Groups*, John Wiley, 1958, New York

SCHEIN, E H, *Organizational Psychology*, Prentice-Hall, 1965, Englewood Cliffs, NJ

SCHEIN, E H and BENNIS, W G, *Personal and Organizational Change Through Group Methods: The Laboratory Approach*, Wiley, 1965, New York

SCOTT, W H, *Industrial Leadership and Joint Consultation*, Liverpool University Press, 1952

SHENFIELD, B E, *Company Boards: their responsibilities to shareholders, employers and the community*, George Allen and Unwin, 1971

SHERIF, M, *An Outline of Social Psychology*, Harper & Row, 1948, New York

SHIMMIN, SYLVIA, 'Postscript—A 1968 Survey of Recent Literature' in MARRIOTT, R, *Incentive Payment Systems*, 3rd rev edn, Staples Press, 1968

SILVERMAN, D, *The Theory of Organization*, Heinemann, 1970

SMITH, P C, 'The prediction of individual differences in susceptibility to industrial monotony', *Journal of Applied Psychology*, 39, 322–29, 1955

SOFER, C, *Men in Mid-Career*, CUP, 1970

STAGNER, R, and ROSEN, H, *The Psychology of Union-Management Relations*, Tavistock Publications, 1965

STEWART, R, *Managers and Their Jobs*, Macmillan, 1967

Swedish Employers Confederation (SAF), *The Condemned Piecework*, SAF, 1972, Stockholm

TABB, J Y, and GOLDFARB, A, *Workers' Participation in*

Management: expectations and experience, Pergamon Press, 1970

TANNENBAUM, A S, *Social Psychology of the Work Organization,* Tavistock Publications, 1966

TANNENBAUM, A S, and ALLPORT, F H, 'Personality structure and group structure: an interpretive study of their relationship through an event-structure hypothesis', *J of Abnormal & Social Psychology,* 53, 272–80, 1956

TANNENBAUM, R, WESCHLER, I R, and MASSARIK, F, *Leadership and Organization: a behavioural science approach,* McGraw-Hill, 1961, New York

TAYLOR, F W, *Scientific Management,* Harper, 1947, New York

THOMASON, G F, *The Management of Research and Development,* Batsford, 1970

THOMPSON, J D, *Organization in Action,* McGraw-Hill, 1967, New York

THOMPSON, J D, and TUDEN, A, 'Strategies, Structures and Process of Organizational Design' in J D Thompson, et al (eds) *Comparative Studies in Administration,* University of Pittsburg Press, 1959, Pittsburg

TILLET, A, KEMPNER, T, and WILLS, G, (eds), *Management Thinkers,* Penguin, 1970

TOLMAN, E C, *Purposive Behaviour in Animals & Men,* Appleton-Century, 1932, New York

Trades Union Congress, *Trade Unionism,* TUC, 1966

TRIST, E L, and BAMFORTH, K W, 'Some social and psychological consequences of the Longwall method of coal getting', *Human Relations,* 4, No. 1, 1951

TRIST, E L, HIGGIN, G W, MURRAY, H, and POLLOCK, A B, *Organizational Choice,* Tavistock Publications, 1963

TURNER, A N, and LAWRENCE, P R, *Industrial Jobs and the Worker,* Harvard University Press, 1965

TURNER, H A, Evidence to Royal Commission on Trade Unions and Employers Associations, *Minutes of Evidence,* No. 364,260, HMSO, 1966

TURNER, H A, 'Is Britain Really Strike Prone?' *Occasional Paper No* 20, Dept of Applied Economics, CUP, 1969, Cambridge

VITELES, M S, *Motivation and Morale in Industry,* W W Morton & Co, 1953, New York

VROOM, V H, *Some Personality Determinants of the Effects of Participation,* Prentice-Hall, 1960, Engelwood Cliffs, NJ

VROOM, V H, *Work and Motivation,* Wiley, 1964, New York

VROOM, V H, and DECI, E J, (eds), *Management and Motivation,* Penguin, 1970

WALKER, C R, 'The problem of the repetitive job', *Harvard Business Review,* 28(3), 54–58, 1950

WALKER, C R, and GUEST, R H, *The Man on the Assembly Line,* Harvard University Press, 1952, Cambridge, Mass

WALKER, C R, (ed), *Modern Technology and Civilisation: An Introduction to Human Problems in the Machine Age,* McGraw-Hill, 1962, New York

WALKER, K F, 'Workers', participation in management: concepts and reality', delivered to the Second World Congress of the International Industrial Relations Association

WALKER, K, 'Industrial Democracy: fantasy, fiction or fact?', The Times Management Lecture, *The Times,* 1970

WALKER, K, and GREYFIE DE BELLECOMBE, L, 'The Concept and its Implementation', *International Institute for Labour Studies, Bulletin,* No. 2, February 1967

WALL, T D, and STEPHENSON, G M, 'Herzberg's two-factor theory of job attitudes: a critical evaluation and some fresh evidence', *Industrial Relations,* 41–65, 1971

WALL, T D, STEPHENSON, G M, and SKIDMORE, C, 'Ego involvement and Herzberg's two factor theory of job satisfaction: an experimental field study', *Brit J of Social and Clinical Psychology,* 10, 23–36, 1971

WALTON, R E, and MCKERSIE, R B, *A Behavioural Theory of Labor Negotiations,* McGraw-Hill, 1965, New York

WEBB, E J, CAMPBELL, D T, SCHWARTZ, R D, and SECHREST, L, *Unobtrusive Measures: Nonreactive Research in the Social Sciences,* Rand McNally & Co, 1966, Chicago

WEBB, S and B, *History of Trade Unionism,* Longmans, 1920

WEBER, M, *The Protestant Ethic and the Spirit of Capitalism,* Allen & Unwin, 1930

WEED, E D, 'Job Enrichment "Cleans Up" at Texas Instruments', MAHER, J R, (ed) *New Perspectives in Job Enrichment,* Van Nostrand Reinhold, 1971

WHITSETT, D A, and WINSLOW, E K, 'An analysis of studies critical of the motivation hygiene theory', *Personnel Psychology,* 20, 391–415, 1967

WHYTE, W F, *Money and Motivation: An Analysis of Incentives in Industry,* Harper & Bros, 1955, New York

WICKERT, F R, 'Turnover and employees' feelings of ego-involvement in the day to day operations of a company', *Personnel Psychology,* 4, 185–97, 1951

WILD, R, 'Job Design Research', Management Centre, University of Bradford, 1970

WILKINS, L T, 'Incentives and the young worker', *Occupational Psychology,* 23, 235–47, 1949

WILKINS, L T, 'Incentives and the young male worker in England', *International J of Opinion & Attitude Research,* 4, 541–62, 1950

WILKINSON, A, *A Survey of Some Western European Experiments in Motivation,* unpublished report prepared by the Institute of Work Study Practitioners, 1971, Enfield, Middx

WILLIAMS, R, and GUEST, D, 'Psychological research and industrial relations: a brief review', *Occupational Psychology,* 43, 201–11, 1969

WIRDENIUS, H, *Supervisors at Work: descriptions of supervisory behaviour,* Garviska Konstanstalten, 1958, Stockholm

WOODWARD, J, *Industrial Organization: Theory and Practice,* OUP, 1965

WOODWARD, J, (ed), *Industrial Organization: Behaviour and Control,* OUP, 1970

ZWEIG, F, *Productivity and Trade Unions,* Blackwell, 1951

INDEX

AUTHOR INDEX

IPM Publishing

Management Paperbacks
Management in Perspective
Handbooks
Surveys

Four series with something to interest *you*. Write for a free copy of our full catalogue: new titles are added regularly. Some of our publications are described overleaf.

IPM Courses and Conferences

A comprehensive programme of courses, seminars and conferences, ranging from basic procedures to the latest techniques and developments, is run throughout the year. The autumn National Conference is the largest management conference in the UK. Other major events are the annual London spring conference and the biennial International Conference which attracts delegates from all over the world.

For a free catalogue or course and conference calendar, please write to IPM at the address on the title page.

IPM Publishing

Job Motivation and Job Design

R Cooper, £1.25; 80p IPM members

"Economic affluence has led to a diminished concern with satisfying basic needs. Improvements in the extent and quality of education, along with the erosion of traditional patterns of authority, are leading people to think increasingly in terms of satisfying their higher order needs, particularly those of self-actualization and self-determination.

"As a result, we are beginning to ask much more from our organizations; instead of simply serving them, we want to know how they can contribute to the quality of our work experience and personal development."

Dr Cooper considers models of motives, job characteristics that motivate, forms of job design, job design as planned change and some ramifications of 'post-industrialism'.

Improving the Quality of Organization

G F Thomason, £1.00; 75p IPM members

Professor Thomason points out that most modern techniques for securing performance and holding the organization together, often conceived in terms of the dynamic functions of management, are rarely seen to require changes in organization if they are to be successful. He considers the quality of organization under four main headings: organizational design and the manager; corporate management; organization of work activity and the organization of administrative management.

Approaches to Supervisory Development

Keith Thurley and Hans Wirdenius, £1.00; 75p IPM members

It has been widely realized that general solutions to supervisory questions probably do not exist; what remains is the thorny question of deciding which policy and which approach is most relevant to the situation in hand. This publication is focused on that problem and aims to provide a set of guidelines for management policy decisions by drawing on recent European research studies.